More than 50 online business ideas

business ideas

A book full of ideas and inspiration to help
get you started with your online business

Staffan Öfwerman

TABLE OF CONTENTS

TABLE OF CONTENTS

Staffan Öfwerman, the author of this book about making money online has a diverse background in music, art, and technology. Introduced to computers in the early 80s, he worked as a computer teacher and also coded a customer relationship management (CRM) software, all alone, for a record club in the mid-80s, selling jazz vinyl records and CDs to its members. Later, he pursued a career in music and also running a couple of popular websites online as a hobby.

As a musician, Staffan has toured and recorded with various artists, but his most notable work was with the legendary duo Roxette in the late 80s and early 90s. He was part of the band behind the two artists during their world tours and he also contributed to their recordings. Staffan's creativity have been evident throughout his music career and these qualities are also reflected in his other activities.

While still passionate about music, Staffan has, for several years, been working with final art for a company in Stockholm, Sweden, where he continued to explore his creativity. As a hobby, he releases his own songs on various streaming platforms under his own name (Staffan Öfwerman). So check it out.

There is also an autobiography released by Staffan about his life in the music business. Get your own copy of "Your Backstage Pass To My Life in Music" at manovermusic.com/book

But now, back to the book you are reading now. Staffan has put together the content for this book, which aims to provide practical tips and insights for readers to find their own niche in the online world and build successful businesses. His background in music, art, and other creative fields allows him to offer a unique perspective on the subject. Through this book, Staffan hopes to inspire readers to take action and explore their own creative ideas, using the book as a tool and a guide to help them achieve their financial goals.

Are you sick and tired of fighting to make ends meet and live paycheck to paycheck? Do you dream of generating extra money while staying at home? If so, you're not by yourself. The good news is that there are a ton of options to make money online on the internet, and this book outlines over 50 various ways to do so.

You don't need to be an expert to start earning money online, which is one of its wonderful features. Anyone can get started thanks to this book's simple explanations and examples. The internet offers countless options to work from home, whether you want to do it part-time or full-time. The internet offers countless options to work from home, whether you are looking to boost your income in your spare time or make it your full-time business.

The potential rewards are typically worth the effort and patience required to make money online. Imagine being able to work independently and from any location. This book offers advice on how to evaluate your interests and skills so that you can pick the best strategy for maximizing your profits.

Some of the businesses or websites mentioned in the book may seem like very large companies and something you cannot achieve yourself, but remember that these companies once started from scratch. Some may have had a unique idea, but others may have simply improved on another service that was already available and instead became market leaders. Therefore, consider that your idea may also lead to something great. However, it requires a lot of hard work and patience. And of course, a bit of luck as well.

Don't let financial problems stop you from living the life you deserve. With the help of the internet you can probably start earning money from home today. This book is a guide to a more satisfying future. So, what are you waiting for? Start exploring the things the internet has to offer and begin your journey towards financial freedom.

This book is your guide to a better future.

Starting your online business is a fulfilling journey, letting you earn money while following your passions. It takes courage and dedication to step out of your comfort zone, but the independenc of working for yourself, from any location, make it worthwhile.

In this book, you will find a variety of ideas and inspiration to help you start your own online business. It's important to read through the entire book to get an idea of the various types of businesses you can start. Keep in mind that the websites mentioned in this book were available at the time it was written, and numbers and prices may differ. Nonetheless, reading about all types of businesses mentioned in the book can still be a great source of inspiration and can help plant a seed that may grow within you.

In this book, you will find a variety of ideas and inspiration to launch your online business. It's important to read through the entire book to get an idea of the various business types you can start. Keep in mind that website details may change, but reading about all types of businesses mentioned can inspire your entrepreneurial journey.

Perhaps there's something within these texts that will really ignite your imagination. It may spark an idea about working with something that's not explicitly mentioned in the book. Instead, just reading about a completely different topic covered within these pages could lead to an entirely new concept. After all, the material presented is only a small piece of what you're capable of. The possibilities are infinite!

It's important take action when you realize there's something you need to learn. Don't wait until tomorrow, since it's easy to get distracted by other things. It's time to make your dreams a reality today by taking the first step towards your dream. Remember that every small step counts and that it's better to move forward with baby steps than not at all.

For added value, visit my website's dedicated page with direct links to book-mentioned companies and resources. I strive to maintain updated links for your convenience. Just go to makeitworkforme.com

I'd be happy to hear about your adventure and to tell others about it. Every entrepreneur has a special story that should be shared. I'd be pleased to look at your online business if it's available on the internet and perhaps feature it on my website, makeitworkforme.com. This will be shown to an audience that includes book readers who might be interested in what you are offering. Additionally, being highlighted on my website might increase your visibility and draw in more visitors/customers. So please don't hesitate to contact me if you've launched your own online business as a result of reading this book and would like to share your experience with others.

makeitworkforme.com

A terrific approach to work from home, set your own hours, and pursue a career you love is to launch an online freelance business. A step-by-step manual for starting a freelance business is provided below:

Step 1: Determine your skills and niche

The first step is to determine your skills and niche. You need to determine your areas of strength and the services you can provide to potential customers. Any ability you have that may be paid for could be used, including writing, graphic design, web programming, social media management, and more.

Step 2: Create a portfolio

Making a portfolio of your work and accomplishments is the next step. Use platforms like Behance, Dribbble, or LinkedIn to showcase your portfolio. Include background information for each project and make sure to highlight your best work.

Step 3: Establish your brand

Building your brand is essential for bringing in customers and developing a reputation. You must have a credible website that displays your offerings, portfolio, and contact details. Create a logo that fits your brand and select a name that accurately describes your company.

Step 4: Set Your rates and payment method

You must decide on your rates and payment alternatives if you want to build a profitable freelance business. You need to do a market research and select pricing that are reasonable and reflect your level of expertise. Your customers can pay using different payment options like PayPal, Stripe and Payoneer.

Step 5: Find clients

Finding clients is the most crucial step in the freelancing process. You can use a websites like Upwork, Freelancer, Fiverr or LinkedIn to find clients. Through social media or email, you can immediately contact prospective customers. Building a successful freelance business requires networking and developing relationships with clients. Through social media or email, you can immediately contact prospective customers. Building a successful freelance business requires networking and developing relationships with clients.

Step 6: Manage your business

You must properly manage your company as it grows. You must keep an eye on your tasks, bills, and payments. To manage your projects and automate your accounting procedures, you can use a variety tools, such as Trello, Asana, or QuickBooks.

Examples of successful freelancing businesses:

Marcos Rezende is a UX Designer from Ontario, Canada, with more than 13 years of experience. He has worked in various industry sectors for multinational organizations in countries like the United States, Canada, Germany, and Brazil. Some of his notable projects include apps for Ontario's COVID-19 dashboard, Urban Master Planning collaboration platform, and Reaction (a kid's e-learning app).

Laura Belgray - Laura is a copywriter who showcases her skills through her website, Talking Shrimp. Her site is a testament to her copywriting abilities, with engaging content throughout, from landing page copy to samples of her client work.

Gary LeMasson - Gary is an SEO expert who has designed his portfolio to resemble Google search results, which is both cheeky and highly relevant for his niche.

Finally, creating an internet freelance business might be a terrific opportunity to create a career doing what you enjoy. You can create a lucrative freelancing business and benefit from being your own boss by following the above-mentioned procedures.

Online surveys are a reliable source of genuine income. Even while it might not be a full-time job, it can be a reliable source of extra income. A step-by-step tutorial on how to launch an internet business doing online surveys is provided below:

Step 1: Research survey sites
The first step is to research and find legitimate survey sites. There are many survey sites out there, but not all of them are legitimate. Look for sites that have a good reputation and pay their users on time. Some examples of reputable survey sites include Swagbucks, Branded Surveys and LifePoints.

Step 2: Sign up for survey sites
Once you have identified legitimate survey sites, sign up for them. You will need to provide basic information like your name, email and demographic information. Some survey sites may require you to complete a profile questionnaire to match you with surveys that fit your interests and demographics.

Step 3: Complete surveys
Once you have signed up for survey sites, start completing surveys. You will receive invitations to participate in surveys based on your profile and demographics. Make sure you complete surveys accurately and honestly as survey sites have quality control mechanisms to detect fraudulent responses.

Step 4: Cash out
Once you have accumulated a certain amount of points or cash, you can cash out your earnings. Different survey sites have different cash-out options, such as PayPal, gift cards or direct deposit. Make sure you understand the cash-out options before you start taking surveys.

Step 5: Maximize your earnings
To maximize your earnings, sign up for multiple survey sites and complete surveys regularly. Some survey sites also offer bonuses and incentives for completing surveys. Look for these opportunities and take advantage of them to earn more.

Examples of successful online survey businesses:

Swagbucks - Swagbucks is a popular survey site that pays users for taking surveys, watching videos, and shopping online. They have paid out over $500 million to their users.

Branded Surveys - Branded Surveys is a renowned survey platform that rewards users for participating in surveys. They have established a strong reputation for their user-friendly interface and diverse range of survey topics.

LifePoints - LifePoints is another leading survey site that offers users the opportunity to earn points by completing surveys. These points can be redeemed for various rewards. LifePoints is known for its wide variety of surveys and its commitment to providing a seamless experience for its users.

In conclusion, taking online surveys is a legitimate way to earn money online. While it may not make you rich, it can be a good source of additional income. By following the steps outlined above, you can start a business online taking surveys and enjoy the benefits of working from home.

Making an internet store is a practical method to turn your hobby into a successful business. You can launch an internet store with ease and start making money right away if you have the correct tools and plan. The steps you can take to launch your own internet store are as follows:

Step 1: Decide on a product or niche

The first step in starting an online store is deciding on a product or niche. You can sell physical products, digital products or a combination of both. You can also choose to focus on a specific niche, such as health and wellness, fashion or home decor.

Step 2: Choose an ecommerce platform

Once you have decided on the products you want to sell, it's time to choose an ecommerce platform. There are many options available, including Shopify, WooCommerce and BigCommerce. These platforms provide you with all the tools you need to build and manage your online store.

Step 3: Set up your online store

After you have chosen an ecommerce platform, it's time to set up your online store. This involves choosing a domain name, designing your website and adding your products. Make sure to choose a user-friendly design and provide clear product descriptions and high quality images.

Step 4: Set up payment and shipping options

In order to sell products online, you need to set up payment and shipping options. Your ecommerce platform will provide you with options to accept payments and handle shipping. Make sure to choose a secure payment gateway and reliable shipping methods.

Step 5: Promote your online store

Once your online store is up and running, it's time to promote it to attract customers. You can use social media, email marketing and search engine optimization (SEO) to drive traffic to your website. You can also use paid advertising to reach a wider audience.

Examples of successful online stores include:

Glossier - a beauty brand that sells skincare and makeup products online.

Warby Parker - an eyewear brand that sells prescription glasses and sunglasses online.

MVMT - a watch and accessory brand that sells products online.

Chewy - an online pet store that sells food, toys and accessories for pets.

Allbirds - a sustainable shoe brand that sells shoes online.

In conclusion, starting an online store is a great way to turn your passion into a profitable business. By following the steps outlined above and choosing the right products and ecommerce platform, you can easily start your own online store and begin generating income.

Affiliate marketing is a type of company where you market other people's goods and be paid a fee for each sale that results from your recommendation. Here is a step-by-step tutorial for beginning an internet affiliate marketing business:

Step 1: Choose a niche

The first step is to choose a niche that you are interested in and passionate about. This could be anything from health and wellness to technology or fashion. Make sure you choose a niche that has a large audience and is profitable.

Step 2: Join affiliate programs

Once you have chosen a niche, you need to join affiliate programs that offer products in that niche. Some examples of affiliate programs include Amazon Associates, ClickBank and ShareASale. Choose affiliate programs that offer products that are relevant to your niche and have a good reputation.

Step 3: Build a website

To promote affiliate products, you need to have a website where you can create content and place your affiliate links. You can either create a website from scratch using platforms like WordPress or use website builders like Wix or Squarespace.

Step 4: Create content

Once you have a website, you need to create high quality content that is relevant to your niche and promotes affiliate products. This could be in the form of blog posts, videos or social media posts. Make sure your content is valuable, informative and engaging to your audience.

Step 5: Promote your content

To drive traffic to your website and promote your affiliate products, you need to promote your content. This could be through social media, paid advertising or search engine optimization (SEO). Choose the promotion methods that work best for your niche and target audience.

Step 6: Monitor your results

As you start promoting affiliate products, it's important to monitor your results and track your earnings. Most affiliate programs offer reporting tools that allow you to see how many clicks and sales your affiliate links are generating. Use this data to optimize your content and promotional strategies.

Examples of successful affiliate marketing businesses:

Smart Passive Income - Smart Passive Income is a website and podcast run by Pat Flynn that teaches people how to start and grow their online businesses. Pat uses affiliate marketing to promote products and services that are relevant to his audience, such as web hosting and email marketing services.

The Wirecutter - The Wirecutter is a website that provides in-depth reviews of products in various niches, such as home and garden, electronics and health and fitness. They use affiliate marketing to earn commissions on the products they recommend.

The Points Guy - The Points Guy is a website that helps people earn and maximize credit card rewards and travel points. They use affiliate marketing to promote credit cards and travel services that are relevant to their audience.

Niche Pursuits - Niche Pursuits is a website created by Spencer Haws that covers case studies, tutorials, and tools to help individuals build niche websites and use affiliate marketing to monetize them.

Just a Girl and Her Blog - Abbie Lawson runs this platform, which offers guidance on organizing, decorating, blogging, and lifestyle topics. Through her site, she recommends various products via affiliate marketing, particularly in the realms of organizing and home decor.

In conclusion, affiliate marketing is a great way to earn money online by promoting other people's products. By following the steps outlined above, you can start an affiliate marketing business and earn a passive income online. Just remember to choose a profitable niche, join reputable affiliate programs, create high quality content, promote your content and monitor your results.

Online blogging can be a great way to make money while sharing your interests, knowledge, and ideas with a larger audience. Here is a step-by-step tutorial on how to launch an internet blogging business:

Step 1: Choose your niche
The first step is to choose a niche that you are passionate about and that has a large audience. Make sure the niche you select is one you have experience in and that you find interesting to write about.

Step 2: Choose a blogging platform
There are many different blogging platforms available like WordPress, Squarespace and Wix. Choose a platform that you find user-friendly, customizable and offers the features you need for your blogging business.

Step 3: Choose a domain name and hosting
Once you have chosen a platform, you need to choose a domain name and hosting for your blog. Your domain name should be relevant to your niche and easy to remember. Hosting is the service that allows your blog to be accessed on the internet.

Step 4: Set up your blog
Once you have a domain name and hosting, you can set up your blog using your chosen platform. Customize your blog's design and layout to make it visually appealing and user-friendly.

Step 5: Create high quality content
To attract readers and build an audience for your blog, you need to create high quality content that is relevant to your niche. This could be in the form of blog posts, videos, podcasts or social media posts. Make sure your content is valuable, informative and engaging to your audience.

Step 6: Promote your blog
To drive traffic to your blog and attract a wider audience, you need to promote your content. This could be through social media, email marketing, search engine optimization (SEO) or guest posting on other blogs. Choose the promotion methods that work best for your niche and target audience.

Step 7: Monetize your blog
Once you have built an audience for your blog, you can start monetizing it by earning income through advertising, affiliate marketing, sponsored content or selling digital products. Choose the monetization methods that are relevant to your niche and that align with your values and goals.

Examples of successful blogging businesses:

The Blonde Abroad - The Blonde Abroad is a travel blog run by Kiersten Rich that provides travel tips, guides and inspiration for women. Kiersten monetizes her blog through affiliate marketing, sponsored content and selling digital products such as travel guides.

Pinch of Yum - Pinch of Yum is a food blog run by Lindsay and Bjork Ostrom that provides recipes, tutorials and food photography tips. They monetize their blog through advertising, sponsored content and selling digital products such as cookbooks and courses.

Smashing Magazine - Smashing Magazine is a web design and development blog that provides tutorials, resources and inspiration for designers and developers. They monetize their blog through advertising, sponsored content and selling digital products such as ebooks and courses.

Fit Men Cook - Fit Men Cook is a health and wellness blog founded by Kevin Curry. He offers healthy, budget-friendly recipes to promote better eating habits. Kevin has successfully monetized his blog through sponsored content, selling his own mobile app, and affiliate marketing.

In conclusion, starting a blogging business online requires choosing a profitable niche, setting up a user-friendly and customizable blogging platform, creating high quality content, promoting your blog and monetizing it through relevant and ethical methods. By following the steps outlined above and learning from successful examples, you can start a blogging business that allows you to share your passion and generate income online.

Anyone who has a love for teaching and wants to make a difference in the lives of students may consider starting an online tutoring business. Here is a step-by-step tutorial on how to launch an online tutoring business:

Step 1: Choose your niche

The first step is to choose your niche. Decide which subjects or skills you want to teach and determine your target audience. You can either specialize in a particular subject such as math, science or English or offer tutoring services for a wide range of subjects.

Step 2: Develop your curriculum

Once you have chosen your niche, develop your curriculum. This involves creating lesson plans, practice materials and quizzes. Make sure your curriculum is engaging, interactive and tailored to the needs of your students.

Step 3: Choose your platform

There are several online tutoring platforms that you can use to connect with students, such as Zoom, Skype or Google Meet. Choose the platform that is most suitable for your needs and your target audience.

Step 4: Set up your website

To promote your tutoring services and attract new clients, you need to set up a professional website. Your website should include information about your services, your credentials and testimonials from satisfied clients. You can use website builders such as Wix or WordPress to create your website.

Step 5: Promote your services

To attract new clients, you need to promote your tutoring services. You can use social media platforms such as Facebook, Twitter and LinkedIn to reach out to potential clients. You can also advertise your services on online tutoring directories such as Tutor.com, TutorMe, or Preply.

Step 6: Offer free trials

To build trust with potential clients and showcase your expertise, offer free trial sessions. This will allow you to demonstrate your teaching skills and connect with potential clients.

Step 7: Set your rates

Once you have established your tutoring business, it's time to set your rates. Research the market rates for tutoring services in your niche and set your rates accordingly. You can either charge by the hour or by the session.

Examples of successful online tutoring businesses:

Skooli - Skooli is a prominent online tutoring platform that offers personalized tutoring sessions across various subjects. They utilize advanced technology to ensure that students are matched with qualified tutors who can cater to their specific academic needs.

Varsity Tutors - Varsity Tutors is an online tutoring platform that offers one-on-one tutoring services in a wide range of subjects.
They use advanced technology to connect students with the best tutors and have received positive reviews from satisfied clients.

Wyzant - Wyzant is a trusted online tutoring platform that connects students with expert tutors in a multitude of subjects. They provide a platform where students can find the perfect tutor based on their learning preferences and requirements.

Mathnasium - Mathnasium is an online tutoring platform that specializes in math tutoring. They offer personalized tutoring services and have helped thousands of students improve their math skills.

In conclusion, starting a business with online tutoring requires choosing your niche, developing your curriculum, choosing your platform, setting up your website, promoting your services, offering free trials and setting your rates. By following the steps outlined above and learning from successful examples, you can start a successful online tutoring business that allows you to make a difference in the lives of students while generating income.

Starting an online social media management firm could be a great business opportunity for people who have experience with social media and have a good sense of branding. Listed below is a step-by-step tutorial on how to launch an online social media management business:

Step 1: Develop your skills and expertise
Before starting a social media management business, it's important to develop your skills and expertise in social media marketing. This can include learning about different social media platforms, creating engaging content, analyzing data and staying up to date with the latest trends and best practices.

Step 2: Define your services
This can include creating social media content, managing social media accounts, analyzing social media data and developing social media marketing strategies. Determine your pricing, packages and deliverables.

Step 3: Choose your target market
Identify your target market. This can include small businesses, startups, entrepreneurs, influencers or any other individual or organization that needs social media management services.

Step 4: Set up your business
Create a business plan, register your business and set up your website. Your website should include information about your services, your pricing, your portfolio and your contact information. You can use website builders such as Wix or WordPress to create your website.

Step 5: Build your portfolio
To attract clients, you need to build a strong portfolio. Create social media accounts for your business, post engaging content and showcase your expertise. You can also offer free social media management services to local businesses to gain experience and build your portfolio.

Step 6: Promote your business
To attract clients, you need to promote your social media management business. Use social media platforms such as Facebook, Twitter, Instagram and LinkedIn to showcase your expertise and connect with potential clients. You can also advertise your services on freelance platforms such as Upwork or Fiverr.

Step 7: Establish your brand
Establish your brand by creating a logo, a brand message and a consistent visual identity. This will help you stand out from your competitors and create a strong brand identity.

Examples of successful social media management businesses:

Hootsuite - Hootsuite is a social media management platform that helps businesses manage their social media accounts and campaigns. They offer a wide range of services, including social media scheduling, monitoring and analytics.

Emplifi - Emplifi (formerly known as Socialbakers) is a social media marketing platform that helps businesses optimize their social media marketing strategies. They offer advanced analytics, competitive insights and influencer marketing services.

Sprout Social - Sprout Social is a social media management platform that helps businesses manage their social media accounts, analyze data and engage with their audience. They offer a range of features, including scheduling, monitoring and reporting.

In conclusion, starting a social media management business online requires developing your skills and expertise, defining your services, choosing your target market, setting up your business, building your portfolio, promoting your business and establishing your brand. By following the steps outlined above and learning from successful examples, you can start a successful social media management business that helps businesses achieve their social media marketing goals.

A successful business can be built using YouTube to capitalize on your interests or talents. Here is a step-by-step tutorial on how to launch an online YouTube business:

Step 1: Define your niche

The first step in starting a YouTube business is to define your niche. Choose a topic that you are passionate about and have expertise in and that has a demand among your target audience. This can include anything from cooking, beauty, fashion, gaming, music or education.

Step 2: Create a YouTube channel

Create a YouTube channel and customize it with a profile picture, cover photo and description. Make sure to choose a name that reflects your niche and is easy to remember.

Step 3: Create high quality content

Create high quality content that engages your audience and provides value. Invest in good equipment, such as a camera, microphone and lighting, to ensure your videos look and sound professional. Consistency is key, so create a content calendar and publish videos regularly.

Step 4: Build your audience

Build your audience by promoting your channel on social media platforms, collaborating with other YouTubers in your niche and engaging with your audience through comments and social media. Respond to comments and feedback and ask for suggestions and ideas for future content.

Step 5: Monetize your channel

Once you have built a following, you can monetize your channel. This can include advertising revenue, sponsorships, merchandise sales or offering premium content or services. You can also join YouTube's Partner Program, which allows you to earn money from ads displayed on your videos.

Step 6: Collaborate with brands

Collaborate with brands that align with your niche and audience. Reach out to brands or agencies that work with influencers or sign up for influencer marketing platforms such as AspireIQ or Influencer.co to find brand collaborations.

Step 7: Analyze your data

Analyze your data to measure your success and improve your strategy. Use YouTube's analytics to track your audience demographics, engagement metrics and revenue. Use this data to refine your content strategy, target your audience better and increase your revenue.

Examples of successful YouTube businesses:

Rosanna Pansino - Rosanna Pansino is a YouTuber who started her YouTube channel, Nerdy Nummies, in 2010. She creates baking tutorials and has over 13 million subscribers. She has since written multiple cookbooks and has her own baking line.

PewDiePie - PewDiePie, whose real name is Felix Kjellberg, is a YouTuber who has been active since 2010. He creates content related to video games and has over 110 million subscribers. He has also released his mobile game, PewDiePie's Tuber Simulator.

Tati Westbrook (Tati) - Tati Westbrook, known simply as Tati on YouTube, is a prominent beauty YouTuber who started her channel in 2010. She reviews beauty products, creates makeup tutorials, and offers insights into the world of cosmetics. Over the years, Tati has amassed a significant following and has even launched her own line of beauty products.

In conclusion, starting a YouTube business online requires defining your niche, creating high quality content, building your audience, monetizing your channel, collaborating with brands and analyzing your data. By following the steps outlined above and learning from successful examples, you can start a successful YouTube business that allows you to turn your passion and creativity into a profitable venture.

Starting an online dropshipping business might be a great way to launch your own business without having to worry about inventory and delivery. A step-by-step tutorial on how to launch a dropshipping business is provided below:

Step 1: Choose a niche

The first step is to select a niche for your dropshipping business. You can use online market research tools to determine popular products and find gaps in the market that you can fill.

Step 2: Find a supplier

Next, you need to find a supplier who will ship products directly to your customers. You can find a supplier by searching online directories like AliExpress, Oberlo or SaleHoo. It's essential to choose a reliable supplier who offers quality products at reasonable prices.

Step 3: Build an online store

Now that you have selected a niche and found a supplier, it's time to create an online store. You can use various eCommerce platforms like Shopify, WooCommerce or BigCommerce to build an online store. Choose a platform that offers easy customization, secure payment options and a user-friendly interface.

Step 4: List products and optimize for SEO

Once your online store is ready, it's time to list products from your supplier. Make sure you optimize your product descriptions and titles for search engines to increase your online visibility.

Step 5: Market your business

Marketing is crucial to the success of your dropshipping business. You can use various channels like social media, content marketing and email marketing to promote your business. Make sure you target the right audience and provide them with quality content that addresses their needs.

Step 6: Manage your business

As your business grows, you need to manage it effectively. You need to keep track of your inventory, customer orders and payments. You can use various tools like QuickBooks or Xero to manage your finances and automate your accounting processes.

Examples of successful dropshipping businesses:

Kylie Cosmetics - Kylie Jenner started her makeup line in 2015 using a dropshipping business model. She partnered with a manufacturer who fulfilled customer orders directly, allowing her to focus on marketing and building her brand.

Oberlo - Oberlo is a popular dropshipping platform that allows e-commerce entrepreneurs to find and sell products without handling inventory or shipping. Starting as a small dropshipping business itself, Oberlo quickly grew in popularity and is now a leading platform integrated with Shopify. It serves as a bridge between e-commerce businesses and suppliers, making dropshipping more accessible for many aspiring entrepreneurs.

Mous - Mous is a phone case brand that started as a dropshipping business on Shopify. They partner with a supplier who manufactures and ships the products directly to customers. Today, they have their own manufacturing facility, but they still use the dropshipping model for some products.

In conclusion, starting a dropshipping business online can be an ideal path to entrepreneurship without the need for significant upfront investments. With the guidelines provided above, you can establish a profitable dropshipping business and relish the perks of being your own boss.

With the proper information, resources, and direction to assist you successfully navigate the market, trading stocks can be a profitable investment opportunity. A step-by-step tutorial on how to launch an online stock trading business is provided here.

Step 1: Educate yourself

The first step in starting a stock trading business is to educate yourself on the basics of trading. There are a lot of online resources available that can help you learn about the stock market, including websites, books, and courses. You should also consider opening a practice account with a broker to practice trading without risking real money.

Step 2: Determine your capital

Before you start trading, you need to determine how much capital you are willing to invest. The amount will depend on your financial goals and risk tolerance. Keep in mind that trading involves risks and you should only invest money that you can afford to lose.

Step 3: Choose a broker

To trade stocks, you will need to open an account with a brokerage firm. There are many online brokerage firms to choose from and each has its own fees, features and tools. Do your research to find a broker that suits your needs and budget.

Step 4: Develop a trading plan

A trading plan is a set of rules that you follow when making trades. Your plan should include your financial goals, risk tolerance and strategies for entering and exiting trades. Stick to your plan to avoid emotional trading, which can lead to poor decision-making and losses.

Step 5: Start trading

Once you have educated yourself, determined your capital, chosen a broker and developed a trading plan, you are ready to start trading. Start small and only trade with the amount of money you can afford to lose. Keep track of your trades and regularly review your trading plan to make adjustments as needed.

Here are a few examples of online brokers you can use to start a stock trading business:

E-Trade: E-Trade is a popular online broker that offers a range of tools and features for traders. They offer a variety of investment options, including stocks, options and mutual funds and have a user-friendly trading platform.

TD Ameritrade: TD Ameritrade is another popular online broker that offers a range of tools and resources for traders. They have a robust trading platform and offer a variety of investment options, including stocks, options and futures.

Robinhood: A newer online broker that offers commission-free trading. They have a simple and easy-to-use trading platform and offer a limited range of investment options, including stocks, options and cryptocurrencies.

In conclusion, starting a stock trading business online requires education, capital, a broker, a trading plan, and a commitment to disciplined trading. With the right tools and guidance, you can start trading stocks and potentially earn a profit.

The Wheel Strategy, which involves selling options online, can be a successful investing strategy, but it necessitates a thorough knowledge of the stock market and options trading. To get started, you can follow the instructions listed below:

Step 1: Educate yourself:
To be successful with The Wheel Strategy, you need to have a deep understanding of the stock market, options trading and how the strategy works. You can do this by taking online courses, reading books, following online resources and attending seminars or workshops. The more knowledge you gain, the better prepared you will be to make informed investment decisions.

Step 2: Open a brokerage account:
After educating yourself, the next step is to choose a reputable online brokerage firm that offers options trading. Some popular brokers include E-Trade, Robinhood, Tastytrade, Interactive Brokers and TD Ameritrade. It's crucial to read their terms and conditions carefully and choose the one that best suits your needs. Make sure to compare fees, trading platforms, research tools and customer support.

Step 3: Fund your account:
Once you've chosen a brokerage firm, fund your account with the amount you're comfortable trading with. It's important to start with a small amount until you gain more experience and confidence in trading. Some brokerage firms may also require a minimum balance to start trading options.

Step 4: Choose your stock:
The Wheel Strategy involves selling options on a stock that you're willing to hold for the long term. It's crucial to choose a stock that you believe will grow over time and even better if it is paying dividends. You can research stocks by analyzing financial statements, industry trends, news and analysts' recommendations.

Step 5: Sell a cash-secured put:
After choosing a stock, you can sell a cash-secured put option at a lower price than the current stock price. This means you're willing to buy the stock at a specific price, known as the strike price, if the option buyer decides to exercise their right. If the stock price goes down, you can buy it at the lower price, which is good. But if the stock price goes up, you keep the money you received for selling the put option.

Step 6: Sell a covered call:

If you were assigned the stocks from selling a put option, you can sell a call option at a higher price than the current stock price. This means you're willing to sell the stock at a specific price, known as the strike price, if the option buyer decides to exercise their right. If the stock price goes up, the call option might be exercised and you can sell the stock at a higher price. But if the stock price stays the same or goes down, you keep the money you received for selling the call option. And if the stock you own also pay dividends, you might also receive dividends while owning the stocks.

Step 7: Repeat the process:

If the call option is assigned, you'll sell the stocks at the strike price. Then you can repeat the process by selling another cash-secured put and later another covered call. The goal is to keep repeating the cycle of selling options and collecting premiums, while also holding onto the stock for the long term while also collecting dividends.

Examples of brokers you can use to start trading The Wheel Strategy:

Tastytrade: Tastytrade is a popular online brokerage firm that offers a range of educational resources, including videos, articles and webinars on options trading.

Robinhood: Robinhood is a commission-free brokerage platform that offers options trading for both beginners and experienced traders. They have a user-friendly app that allows you to easily monitor your trades and make adjustments on the go.

Option Alpha: Option Alpha is an options trading education and training platform that offers a variety of courses, resources and tools to help traders improve their skills and strategies. They have a community forum where you can ask questions and share ideas with other traders.

Interactive Brokers: Interactive Brokers is a global online brokerage firm that offers options trading in a range of markets, including stocks, futures and forex. They provide advanced trading tools and platforms for active traders and investors.

In conclusion, The Wheel Strategy can be a profitable way to invest in the stock market, but it requires a lot of knowledge, experience and discipline. It's important to start with a small amount, choose a reputable brokerage firm, select the right stocks and always do your research. Remember that options trading can be risky and you should never invest more than you can afford to lose. Consult with a financial advisor if you have any doubts or concerns.

Starting a day trading business online can be challenging but lucrative if done correctly. Day traders buy and sell financial products including stocks, currencies, and futures over the course of a single trading day in an effort to turn a profit. Here are steps on how to launch an online day trading business:

Step 1: Develop a trading strategy
Develop a trading strategy that fits your trading style and risk tolerance. Learn from sources such as books, online courses or trading communities.

Step 2: Learn the basics of trading:
It's important to understand the basics of trading before starting your business. You may need to learn how to read financial charts, use technical analysis and understand market psychology.

Step 3: Set up a trading account:
To start trading, you need a trading account with a broker. You should choose an online broker that offers low fees and provides a user-friendly platform.

Step 4: Fund your account
Once you have a trading account, you need to fund it with capital. You can start with a small amount and gradually increase your investment as you gain experience.

Step 5: Choose a niche
You can specialize in a particular market, such as stocks, forex, options, futures or focus on a particular trading style such as scalping, swing trading or position trading.

Step 6: Develop a risk management plan
Risk management is crucial in day trading. You need to have a plan that includes your risk tolerance, stop-loss orders and position sizing. A plan is important. And to stick to the plan is even more important.

Step 7: Practice trading
You should use a demo trading account to practice your trading skills and test your trading strategy without risking real money. Also known as a paper account.

Step 8: Keep a trading journal
Record all your trades, including the entry and exit points, the amount of capital invested and the profit or loss. This will help you analyze your performance and improve your trading strategy.

Step 9: Join a trading community
Joining a trading community can be beneficial as it provides an opportunity to learn from experienced traders, share trading ideas and get feedback on your trades.

Step 10: Stay up-to-date with market news and events
Keep track of the latest market news and events that can impact your trades. You can use financial news websites to stay informed.

Examples of popular online day trading businesses include:

Warrior Trading: a day trading education and chatroom website founded by Ross Cameron. The platform offers a variety of courses, live trading chat rooms and tools for traders of all experience levels. Warrior Trading has a large following on social media and has been featured in major financial news outlets such as Bloomberg and CNN.

Day Trade Ideas: a subscription-based trading service that provides daily market analysis and trading ideas. The company was founded by Jason Sen, who has over 30 years of experience in the financial markets. Day Trade Ideas offers a variety of plans for traders of all levels, from beginner to advanced.

Investopedia Academy: an online education platform that offers courses in finance and investing. The academy has a variety of courses related to day trading, including a course on day trading strategies. The courses are self-paced and taught by experienced instructors.

Bulls on Wall Street: Founded by Kunal Desai, Bulls on Wall Street offers day trading courses, mentorship, and a live trading room. They emphasize hands-on training and provide access to webinars, video lessons, and boot camps. Kunal and his team teach their strategies through live trading and market analysis, assisting both beginners and experienced traders in refining their skills and strategies.

In conclusion, launching an internet day trading business can be a thrilling and perhaps successful career. To succeed, though, you need to put a lot of effort into your research, planning, and discipline. It's critical to educate yourself on the markets, create a trading strategy, and carefully manage your risk. You'll also need the right tools and resources, such as a reliable trading platform and access to current market data. You may develop a great internet business and become a successful day trader by following these steps.

Starting an online bookshop is a terrific way to turn your passion for reading into a successful business. It's now simpler than ever to launch an online bookselling business because to the growth of e-commerce and the rising popularity of online book sales. However, in order to guarantee the success of your organization, a plan must be put in place. The first steps are as follows:

Step 1: Determine Your Niche

To make your online bookstore stand out, it's essential to decide on a niche. Will you specialize in rare and collectible books or will you focus on popular titles in a specific genre? For example, you could choose to sell books in the science fiction and fantasy genre. By determining your niche, you can better target your audience and make your business stand out.

Step 2: Build Your Inventory

Once you know your niche, start building your inventory. You can purchase books from yard sales, thrift stores and online marketplaces like eBay and Amazon. For example, if you choose to specialize in rare and collectible books, you could look for antique bookstores and estate sales to find unique titles. Consider also building relationships with publishers, distributors and other booksellers to obtain inventory at wholesale prices.

Step 3: Set Up Your Online Store

There are several e-commerce platforms to choose from when setting up your online bookselling store. Consider using platforms like Amazon, eBay or AbeBooks. You can also create your own website using platforms like Shopify or WordPress and integrate it with a payment gateway like PayPal and Stripe. For example, if you choose to use Amazon, you'll need to sign up for a seller account and create your product listings.

Step 4: Optimize Your Listings

To increase sales, it's important to optimize your book listings. This includes creating compelling product descriptions, using high quality images and pricing your books competitively. For example, you could include information about the author and a brief summary of the book in the product description.

Step 5: Market Your Business

Once your store is set up, it's time to market your business. Use social media, email marketing and other online advertising channels to drive traffic to your store. You can also reach out to book bloggers and other influencers in your niche to promote your store. For example, you could create social media accounts for your business and post about new book releases, promotions and events.

In terms of what you need to start an online bookselling business, you will need a computer, internet connection, a camera to take pictures of your books and shipping supplies to send your orders. As your business grows, you may also need to invest in software to manage your inventory and finances.

Examples of successful online bookselling businesses:

Thriftbooks: This online bookstore started in 2003 and has grown to become one of the largest sellers of used books online. They offer a wide selection of titles at affordable prices and have a user-friendly website that makes it easy for customers to find what they're looking for.

Powell's Books: This independent bookstore based in Portland oregon, has been selling books online since the early days of the internet. They specialize in rare and out-of-print books and have a large and loyal following of customers who appreciate their commitment to quality and customer service.

Better World Books: This online bookstore has a unique business model that focuses on social and environmental responsibility. They sell used books and donate a portion of their profits to literacy initiatives around the world. They also offer free shipping on all orders, making it easy for customers to support a good cause while shopping for books.

BookOutlet: This online retailer offers discounted books from popular authors and publishers. They have a large selection of books in various genres and their prices are hard to beat. They also have a rewards program that allows customers to earn points for purchases and redeem them for discounts on future orders.

Booktopia: This Australian-based online bookstore offers a wide selection of books, DVDs and CDs at competitive prices. They have a user-friendly website and offer free shipping on orders over a certain amount. They also have a blog that features book reviews and other book-related content, which helps to build a community of book lovers around their brand.

In conclusion, starting an online bookselling business can be a lucrative and rewarding venture for book lovers. By following these steps and staying committed to your business, you can build a successful online store and turn your passion for books into a profitable career.

Starting an online virtual assistant business might be a terrific way to work from home and earn money. You can offer a range of services to clients as a virtual assistant, including bookkeeping, social media management, and administrative help. The following are the steps you can take to launch an online virtual assistant business:

Step 1: Determine your skills and services
The first step is to determine what services you will offer as a virtual assistant. Identify your skills and strengths and research what services are in demand in the market.

Step 2: Set your rates
After identifying your services, set your rates. Research the rates charged by other virtual assistants in your niche and location to determine your pricing.

Step 3: Create a website
A website is a must for any virtual assistant business. It provides a platform to showcase your services and portfolio to potential clients. You can create a website using website builders such as Wix, Squarespace or WordPress.

Step 4: Set up social media profiles
Social media is an important marketing tool for any virtual assistant business. Create profiles on social media platforms such as LinkedIn, Facebook, Twitter and Instagram to connect with potential clients.

Step 5: Network
Networking is crucial in the virtual assistant industry. Attend industry events, join online groups and forums and connect with other virtual assistants to build relationships and gain potential clients.

Step 6: Market your services
Use various marketing strategies to promote your services, such as creating a blog, guest posting on industry websites and reaching out to potential clients via email or social media.

Step 7: Set up systems and processes
To run a successful virtual assistant business, you need to have systems and processes in place to manage your work and clients efficiently. This includes tools such as project management software, time-tracking tools and invoicing software.

Step 8: Find clients
There are several ways to find clients as a virtual assistant, such as using job boards like Upwork or Freelancer, cold pitching to potential clients or partnering with other service providers.

Some examples of virtual assistant services you can offer include:

• Providing administrative support, such as managing emails, scheduling appointments, and handling data entry tasks efficiently.

• Offering comprehensive social media management services, including content creation, strategic post scheduling, and in-depth metric analysis.

• Assisting with bookkeeping and accounting responsibilities, such as professional invoicing, meticulous account reconciliation, and expert tax preparation.

• Delivering high-quality content creation services, including crafting engaging blog posts, producing captivating videos, and creating eye-catching graphics.

• Ensuring top-notch customer service by promptly responding to customer inquiries, addressing their concerns, and managing all aspects of customer interaction.

Examples of websites and resources that can assist you in starting your own virtual assistant business include:

International Virtual Assistants Association (IVAA): The IVAA is a dedicated professional association that provides virtual assistants with essential resources, training, and networking opportunities.

Upwork: A renowned job board, Upwork provides a space for virtual assistants to market their services and connect with potential clients looking for assistance.

Freelancer: Similar to Upwork, Freelancer connects virtual assistants with clients actively seeking assistance, presenting numerous job opportunities.

LinkedIn: As a professional social media platform, LinkedIn is in-valuable for virtual assistants looking to display their skills, network, and establish connections with potential clients.

Horkey Handbook: Founded by Gina Horkey, this platform is a treasure trove for those eager to dive into the world of virtual assistance or freelance writing. It offers courses, a plethora of actionable tips, and a regularly updated blog filled with invaluable insights.

Starting a virtual assistant business online can be a lucrative and flexible way to make money from home. With the right skills, tools and marketing strategies, you can attract clients and build a successful business.

Given the growing need for expert translation services across a range of businesses as a result of globalization, starting an internet translation company can provide a lucrative and adaptable revenue stream. The following is a guide that details the procedures necessary to start an internet translation company:

Step 1: Identify your language pairs and niche

First, identify the language pairs you are proficient in and the areas of expertise you have. This will help you define your target market and specialize in a particular niche. Some examples of niches include legal, medical, technical and marketing translation.

Step 2: Develop your skills

If you want to establish yourself as a professional translator, it's important to have the necessary skills and qualifications. This includes having fluency in your language pairs, a strong understanding of grammar and syntax and experience in your niche. You may also want to consider obtaining a degree
or certification in translation.

Step 3: Set up your business

Once you have identified your language pairs and niche, you'll need to set up your business. This includes deciding on a business name, registering your business and obtaining any necessary licenses or permits. You may also want to set up a website and create social media accounts to promote your services.

Step 4: Build your portfolio

To attract clients, you'll need to build a portfolio of your work. This can include samples of translations you've completed, testimonials from satisfied clients and any relevant certifications or qualifications you have. You may also want to consider offering your services for free or at a discounted rate to build your portfolio and gain experience.

Step 5: Market your services

To attract clients, you'll need to market your services effectively. This can include creating a website that showcases your services, networking with potential clients and using social media to promote your business. You may also want to consider offering a referral program to incentivize satisfied clients to refer their friends and colleagues.

Step 6: Set your rates

It's important to set your rates competitively while still ensuring that you're being compensated fairly for your time and expertise. You may want to research the rates of other translators in your niche and consider factors such as the complexity of the text and the turnaround time when setting your rates.

Step 7: Establish your workflow

Once you have clients, you'll need to establish a workflow to ensure that projects are completed on time and to a high standard. This can include using translation tools such as CAT (computer-assisted translation) software, setting clear expectations with clients regarding deadlines and revisions and using project management tools to track progress.

Examples of successful online translation businesses:

Gengo - Gengo specializes in delivering professional translation services in more than 70 languages, providing a reliable and efficient solution for businesses and individuals seeking to communicate effectively across linguistic barriers.

BLEND Express - BLEND Express, formerly known as One Hour Translation, offers efficient, affordable, and professional online translation and editing services, ensuring quick turnaround times for clients.

ProTranslating - ProTranslating has been in the translation business for over 40 years, specializing in legal, medical and technical translations. Its focus on these specific areas has enabled the company to develop a high level of expertise, making it a trusted name in the industry.

In conclusion, establishing a successful online translation business necessitates dedication, hard work and an unwavering commitment to quality. Building your skills and portfolio is crucial to achieving success and by following the steps outlined above, you can position yourself as a successful online translator and build a thriving business. It is essential to keep in mind that the translation industry is highly competitive, so it is important to continuously improve and effectively market your services to distinguish yourself from the competition.

Starting an online data entry business could be a terrific way to work from home and make money. You only need a computer and an internet connection for this type of business. This is a step-by-step guide on how to start an online data entry business:

Step 1: Determine your skills and services

The first step is to decide what kind of services you will offer. Some common data entry services include data processing, data mining, data cleaning, transcription and data analysis. You can also specialize in a particular industry such as healthcare, finance or legal.

Step 2: Research your market and competitors

Before starting a data entry business, you need to research your target market and competitors. Identify the types of businesses that are most likely to require your services. Also, research your competitors to find out what services they offer, their pricing strategies and their target market.

Step 3: Create a business plan

Creating a business plan is important for any type of business. Your business plan should outline your services, target market, pricing, marketing strategies and financial projections. It should also include your goals and objectives for the business.

Step 4: Set up your home office

To start a data entry business, you probably need a computer, high-speed internet, a printer and a scanner. You should also have a comfortable and quiet home office where you can work without interruptions. Consider investing in a good ergonomic chair and desk to ensure you can work for long hours without getting fatigued.

Step 5: Develop your website and portfolio

Creating a professional website and portfolio is essential for any online business. Your website should showcase your services, pricing and contact information. You should also include a portfolio of your previous work and client testimonials. Consider using a professional web designer to create a unique and appealing website.

Step 6: Market your business

Every business needs marketing to be successful. There are several ways to market your business online, including social media, search engine optimization (SEO) and paid advertising. Joining online forums and professional groups can also help you connect with potential clients and grow your business.

Step 7: Build your client base

Once you have set up your business and marketing strategies, it's time to start building your client base. Reach out to potential clients through email or social media. You can also use freelance job platforms like Upwork, Freelancer and Fiverr to find clients.

Examples of successful online data entry businesses and their services:

Virtual Gal Friday - Virtual Gal Friday specializes in administrative support services, including data entry, bookkeeping and transcription. With a focus on high quality customer service and attention to detail, Virtual Gal Friday has established itself as a trusted partner for clients seeking efficient and reliable data entry solutions.

Clickworker - Clickworker is a renowned platform that offers a variety of online tasks, including data entry, writing, and research. They leverage the power of a vast crowd of Clickworkers who handle these micro-tasks, making it a trusted choice for businesses seeking digital services.

Task Virtual - Task Virtual offers virtual assistant services, including data entry, social media management, and email management. With a team of experienced professionals, Task Virtual provides personalized solutions that meet the unique needs of each client, delivering efficient and accurate results.

SigTrack - SigTrack offers remote data entry jobs, specifically related to petition signatures. This platform often requires users to validate signatures against voter databases, ensuring accuracy in data processing tasks.

Starting a data entry business online requires patience, hard work and dedication. With the right skills and strategies you can probably create a successful and profitable business from the comfort of your own home.

Starting an online coaching business is a fantastic opportunity to share your knowledge with more people and assist them in achieving their goals. This can be the appropriate career choice for you if you are enthusiastic about a particular subject and want to assist others. Here are some recommendations to get you going:

Step 1: Determine your niche
The first step to starting an online coaching business is to determine your niche. Decide on the area you want to specialize in and ensure that it is something you are passionate about. Examples of niches include health and wellness, business coaching, life coaching or relationship coaching.

Step 2: Develop your expertise
To be a successful coach, you need to have expertise in your chosen niche. If you don't have experience or knowledge in your chosen area, you may need to take courses or gain experience to become an expert.

Step 3: Identify your ideal client
Determine the type of person you want to work with and who will benefit the most from your coaching. This will help you target your marketing efforts and attract the right clients.

Step 4: Choose your coaching method
There are many different coaching methods you can choose from, including one-on-one coaching, group coaching or self-paced courses. Consider which method will work best for you and your clients.

Step 5: Set up your website
Create a website that showcases your expertise and services. Ensure that your website is easy to navigate, visually appealing and provides all the necessary information your clients need to know about your services.

Step 6: Develop your brand
Develop a brand that resonates with your target audience. This includes creating a logo, choosing a color palette and designing a website that reflects your brand.

Step 7: Create coaching packages
Develop coaching packages that will appeal to your target audience. Ensure that your pricing is competitive and that your packages offer value to your clients.

Step 8: Develop your marketing strategy
Develop a marketing strategy that will help you reach your target audience. This can include social media marketing, email marketing, content marketing and paid advertising.

Step 9: Build your network
Build relationships with other coaches and entrepreneurs in your industry. This will help you build your network, find potential clients and learn from other successful coaches.

Step 10: Continuously improve your skills
To be a successful coach, you need to continuously improve your skills and knowledge. This includes attending conferences, reading industry publications and staying up-to-date with the latest coaching trends and techniques.

Examples of successful online coaching businesses and their strategies:

Tony Robbins - Tony Robbins is one of the most well-known coaches in the world, with over four decades of experience in the industry. Robbins has built his brand by developing a unique coaching style that combines personal development, psychology and business strategies. He has also leveraged the power of the internet to reach a global audience, offering online courses, webinars and coaching programs.

Marie Forleo - Marie Forleo is a marketing and business coach who has built a successful online business by developing a strong personal brand and leveraging social media. Forleo's coaching style is focused on helping entrepreneurs develop their businesses by combining effective marketing strategies with personal development principles. She offers a range of online courses, webinars and coaching programs and has developed a large following on social media platforms like YouTube and Instagram.

Gabrielle Bernstein - Gabrielle Bernstein is a spiritual coach and author who has built a successful online business by leveraging the power of storytelling and personal branding. Bernstein's coaching style is focused on helping clients connect with their spirituality and develop a deeper sense of purpose in their lives. She has authored several bestselling books, offers online courses and has developed a large following on social media platforms like Instagram and Facebook.

In conclusion, starting an online coaching business requires dedication, hard work and a willingness to continuously improve. With the right strategy and mindset, you can build a successful coaching business that helps people achieve their goals and live their best lives.

You may convert your love of writing into a successful business by starting an online writing business. There are numerous options for freelance writers to make a job online, whether they are interested in copywriting, ghostwriting, or content writing. Here are some instructions on how to begin:

Step 1: Choose your writing niche

The first step in starting an online writing business is to decide on your writing niche. There are many different types of writing niches to choose from, including:

• Content Writing: Creating blog posts, articles and other types of content for websites• Copywriting: Writing marketing materials, such as sales pages, email campaigns and advertisements• Ghostwriting: Writing books, articles or blog posts for clients who will publish it under their name• Technical Writing: Creating user manuals, product descriptions and other technical documents

Step 2: Build your portfolio

Your portfolio is your proof of your writing skills and expertise. This can include writing samples, testimonials from clients and a description of your services. You can build your portfolio by:

• Creating a website: This can be done through website builders such as Wix, WordPress or Squarespace.

• Creating a writing blog: This can be a great way to showcase your writing skills and build an audience.

• Offering free or low-cost writing services: This can help you build your portfolio while gaining experience and making connections in the industry.

Step 3: Set your rates and create a business plan

Once you have built your portfolio, you need to decide on your rates and create a business plan. You should consider factors such as the type of writing you will be doing, the time required for each project and the level of expertise required. To determine your rates, you can research what other freelance writers in your niche are charging and then set your rates accordingly. It's important to remember that as a beginner, you may need to charge lower rates to attract clients and build your reputation. You should also create a business plan that outlines your goals, target market and marketing strategies. This will help you stay focused and organized as you grow your business.

Step 4: Find clients

To find clients, you can:

• Network with other freelance writers and potential clients on social media platforms like LinkedIn, Twitter, or Facebook groups.

• Pitch your services to blogs, magazines and websites that you want to work for.

• Join freelance writing platforms like Upwork, Freelancer or Fiverr, where you can apply for writing jobs and bid on projects.

Step 5: Deliver high quality work and build relationships

Once you've found clients, it's important to deliver high quality work and build strong relationships with them. This will help you gain repeat business and referrals, which can be essential for growing your writing business.

Examples of online writing business:

Freelance Writers Den - Freelance Writers Den by Carol Tice is a community and training center for freelance writers of all levels. Members have access to resources such as job boards, live events and a supportive forum.

Writing Revolt - Writing Revolt by Jorden Roper is an online platform that teaches freelance writers how to start and grow their own writing businesses. Jorden shares her own experiences and strategies for finding clients and earning a steady income.

Freelancer FAQs - Freelancer FAQs by Elna Cain is a resource hub for freelance writers and other online entrepreneurs. Elna provides practical advice and tips on how to start and run a successful online business, including writing, blogging and social media marketing.

In conclusion, starting an online writing business requires determination, hard work and patience. By choosing your writing niche, building your portfolio, setting your rates, finding clients and delivering high quality work, you can build a successful online writing business.

Anyone with experience or a passion in marketing, advertising, or business may find starting a digital marketing business to be a thrilling endeavor. The actions you must take to launch your own digital marketing company are outlined in this guide.

Step 1: Develop your skills and knowledge

You need to understand the aspects of digital marketing before you launch a digital marketing business. This includes SEO, social media marketing, email marketing and web analytics. You can acquire the necessary knowledge through online courses, certification programs, webinars, workshops and practical experience.

Step 2: Define your target audience and services

Determine the clientele you wish to serve and the services you will provide. This will help you in developing a detailed and targeted marketing strategy as well as brand messaging that appeals to your target market.Consider specializing in a particular niche or industry to differentiate yourself from competitors.

Step 3: Choose a business model

There are different business models for digital marketing agencies such as retainer, project-based and performance-based. Determine which model suits your skills, resources and target market.

Step 4: Set up your business

Register your business, create a business plan, set up a website and create social media accounts. Your website should include info about your services, pricing, testimonials and contact information.

Step 5: Build your network

Develop relationships with other professionals and organizations in your industry. Attend networking events, participate in online communities and reach out to potential clients.

Step 6: Create a pricing strategy

Figure out how much you will charge for your services. Consider factors such as your target market, competition, expertise and overhead costs. Develop a pricing strategy that is competitive, profitable and sustainable.

Step 7: Find clients

Utilize diverse marketing channels to effectively reach your intended audience, including social media, email marketing, content marketing, SEO, and PPC advertising. It's also beneficial to establish a collection of case studies and testimonials that demonstrate your proficiency and knowledge. Leverage your network to get referrals and word-of-mouth marketing.

Examples of digital marketing businesses:

Neil Patel Digital: a full-service agency founded by Neil Patel, offering SEO, content marketing, PPC and more. They have helped many businesses increase their online visibility and revenue.

Ignite Digital: a Canadian-based agency that offers a range of digital marketing services, including SEO, social media marketing, PPC and web design. They have a proven track record of driving results.

Disruptive Advertising: a Utah-based PPC agency that specializes in Google Ads, Facebook and LinkedIn advertising. They pride themselves on their data-driven approach to ad optimization and have helped many businesses increase their ROI.

SmartSites: a New Jersey-based agency that offers a range of digital marketing services, including SEO, PPC, web design and e-commerce development. They work with businesses of all sizes and have won numerous awards for their work.

Single Grain: a California-based agency that focuses on growth marketing, helping businesses achieve rapid and sustainable growth through a variety of digital marketing tactics. They have worked with clients such as Uber, Amazon and Salesforce and have a team of experts in areas such as SEO, PPC and content marketing.

Starting a digital marketing company requires perseverance, commitment, and a passion for assisting clients in achieving their business objectives. You can position yourself for success and create a successful digital marketing company by adhering to these steps.

For people with a history in bookkeeping or accounting who want to live a work-from-home lifestyle, starting an online bookkeeping firm is a wise choice. A guide for starting an online bookkeeping business is provided below:

Step 1: Assess your skills and equipment

Before starting an online bookkeeping business, it's important to assess your skills and equipment. You need to have strong accounting skills, knowledge of bookkeeping software and experience with financial analysis. In addition, you'll need a computer, reliable internet connection and accounting software like QuickBooks, Xero or FreshBooks.

Step 2: Choose your services and target market

Once you've assessed your skills and equipment, you need to choose the services you want to offer and the target market you want to serve. You could specialize in basic bookkeeping services, financial statement preparation or tax preparation. Your target market could be small businesses, solopreneurs or freelancers.

Step 3: Develop a business plan

Developing a business plan is essential for any business, including an online bookkeeping business. This plan should include your target market, services offered, pricing, marketing strategy and financial projections. Your business plan will serve as a roadmap for your business and will help you stay focused and organized.

Step 4: Register your business

Before you can start your online bookkeeping business, you need to register it with the appropriate authorities in your state or country. This will typically involve obtaining a business license and registering for taxes.

Step 5: Set up your website and social media presence

In order to market your online bookkeeping business effectively, you'll need to have a professional website and a strong social media presence. Your website should be easy to navigate, visually appealing and include information about your services, pricing and contact information. You should also create profiles on social media platforms like LinkedIn, Twitter and Facebook.

Step 6: Determine your pricing

Pricing is a crucial element of any online bookkeeping business. You need to determine how much you'll charge for your services, taking into account factors like the complexity of the work, the level of expertise required and the amount of time you'll need to devote to each client.

Step 7: Build your client base

Once you've set up your online bookkeeping business, it's time to start building your client base. You can use social media and other online marketing strategies to reach potential clients. You could also offer free consultations or workshops to attract new clients.

Examples of successful online bookkeeping businesses:

Bench.co: Offers online bookkeeping services for small businesses and startups. Their cloud-based software streamlines bookkeeping tasks and provides real-time financial insights.

Bookkeeper.com: Provides online bookkeeping, accounting and payroll services to small and medium-sized businesses. They offer customized bookkeeping solutions tailored to each client's needs.

Bookkeeper360: Specializes in cloud-based bookkeeping services for small businesses, startups and entrepreneurs. Their services include bookkeeping, accounting, tax preparation and financial advisory.

inDinero: Delivers full-service accounting and tax solutions tailored to entrepreneurs and growing businesses. Their comprehensive financial tools, paired with a team of bookkeepers, offer a holistic approach to financial management.

Merritt Bookkeeping: Offers simple, flat-rate online bookkeeping services for small businesses. With a focus on straightforward pricing and clear communication, they provide monthly financial reports to help businesses understand their finances.

By following the example of successful online bookkeeping businesses like Bench, Bookkeeper.com and Bookkeeper360, you can start your own online bookkeeping business and offer a range of bookkeeping services to clients. With the freedom and flexibility of working from home, you can build a successful and profitable business.

If you're someone who loves research and has a knack for it, then starting an internet research company could be a great opportunity for you. Here's a step-by-step guide on how to launch your own research business:

Step 1: Choose your area of specialization

Think about the area of research that interests you the most. It could be anything from market research to academic research, scientific research or competitive analysis. Once you've decided on your niche, you'll be able to focus your efforts better and reach out to potential clients more effectively.

Step 2: Hone your skills

To be successful in the research business, you need a specific set of skills, such as critical thinking, analytical skills, attention to detail, and excellent communication skills. Consider taking courses or getting certified to enhance your skills and increase your credibility.

Step 3: Specify your offerings

Select the services you want to provide as a research company. This can range from gathering and analyzing data to writing reports, conducting literature reviews, and more. You will be able to market your company more successfully if you have a clear and concise list of services.

Step 4: Create a business plan

Develop a comprehensive business plan that outlines your goals, target market, pricing strategy, and marketing plan. A business plan will keep you focused and organized as you build your business.

Step 5: Set up your website

Your website will be the foundation of your online research business. Make sure it's professional, easy to navigate, and showcases your services and expertise. Don't forget to include a contact form, so potential clients can get in touch with you.

Step 6: Build your network

Build a network of contacts who can recommend you to others by contacting potential clients in your niche. To increase your network, go to relevant industry events and think about joining associations.

Step 7: Determine your pricing

Decide on your pricing strategy based on the level of expertise required for your services, your niche, and your competition. You may want to offer different pricing tiers to appeal to a range of clients.

Step 8: Market your business

Create a marketing strategy to advertise your products and strengthen your brand. This can involve producing content for your website, blogging as a guest on websites that are relevant, using social media to market, and using email to market.

Examples of successful online research businesses:

Research Optimus - Offers a variety of research services including data analytics, market research and industry research.

ClearView Research - Offers both qualitative and quantitative research solutions to clients across a wide range of industries, including but not limited to healthcare and technology.

Research Pool - Offers customized research solutions to clients, including market research, data collection and analytics.

Wonder Research: Provides clients with access to a network of researchers who deliver detailed insights and data on a variety of topics, from market trends to competitive analysis.

BCC Research: Specializes in market research reports and industry forecasts across various domains such as health, chemicals, and energy. They provide businesses with the insights needed to make informed decisions.

Starting an online research business can be a challenging yet rewarding venture for individuals with a passion for research. By following these steps and building a solid foundation for your business, you can establish yourself as a trusted research professional and grow your business over time.

For those with design expertise and an entrepreneurial spirit, starting an internet graphic design business might be a lucrative career decision. Here is a step-by-step tutorial for starting an online graphic design business.

Step 1: Assess your skills and determine your niche

First, assess your graphic design skills and determine your niche. Consider what types of design work you enjoy and are proficient in. Some examples of graphic design niches include branding and logo design, web design, print design, packaging design and social media graphics.

Step 2: Define your target market

Once you have determined your niche, define your target market. Consider what types of clients you want to work with and tailor your services and marketing efforts to their needs. For example, if you specialize in branding and logo design, your target market may be small businesses looking to establish their brand identity.

Step 3: Develop your brand and portfolio

Develop your brand and create a portfolio of your best work. Your brand should reflect your design style and appeal to your target market. Your portfolio should showcase your skills and provide examples of your work in your chosen niche.

Step 4: Set your prices and services

Set your prices and determine the services you will offer. Consider the industry standards for pricing and the value of your services. Don't undervalue your work, but also be competitive in your pricing.

Step 5: Build your website and online presence

Build a professional website and create an online presence to showcase your work and attract clients. Your website should include your portfolio, services, pricing and contact information. You can also use social media platforms to connect with potential clients and showcase your work.

Step 6: Market your services

Market your services through various channels, such as social media, email marketing and online advertising. Utilize search engine optimization (SEO) strategies to improve your website's visibility and attract more traffic.

Step 7: Build relationships with clients

Build strong relationships with your clients by delivering high quality work, providing excellent customer service and communicating effectively. Satisfied clients can provide valuable referrals and help grow your business through word-of-mouth.

Graphic Design – Where to start and examples:

Fiverr: Fiverr is a well-known online marketplace where freelancers can offer their graphic design services at low costs, making it an excellent platform to start your business. You can build your portfolio and gain experience while charging affordable rates, which can help you attract more clients in the future.

Upwork: Upwork is another popular platform that connects freelancers with clients. You can create a profile and bid on design projects that match your skills and expertise.

99designs: 99designs is a platform that connects businesses with freelance graphic designers. You can participate in design contests and create custom designs for clients.

Canva: Canva is a free online graphic design tool that allows you to create custom designs for your clients. It's a great tool to use when starting your business, as it's affordable and easy to use.

Wix: Wix is a website builder that offers a range of templates and design tools to help you create a professional website for your graphic design business. It's a great option for those with no coding experience.

In conclusion, starting a graphic design business online requires a combination of design skills, business savvy and marketing know-how. By following the above steps and utilizing the resources and platforms available, you can build a successful graphic design business online.

Starting an online web development business may be a rewarding and successful venture if you have the necessary skills and dedication. Below is a step-by-step guide for getting started:

Step 1: Find your field of expertise
Web development is a vast field and it's crucial to determine which areas you'll focus on. You could specialize in front-end development, back-end development, e-commerce websites, mobile app development or web design, among others.

Step 2: Build your skills
Web development requires a strong foundation in coding languages such as HTML, CSS, JavaScript and PHP, among others. It's essential to have a solid understanding of web design principles, web development frameworks and content management systems.

Step 3: Create a portfolio
A portfolio showcases your skills and abilities to potential clients. Build a portfolio of projects that you've worked on, whether they're personal or for clients.

Step 4: Set up your business
Create a business strategy, pick a name for your company, then register it with the appropriate authorities. Depending on where in the world you live, you might also need to register for taxes and get a company license.

Step 5: Establish your online presence
Build a website for your business, showing your portfolio and services. You can use website builders like WordPress, Wix or Squarespace to create a website with no coding knowledge.

Step 6: Market your services
Identify your target market and develop a marketing strategy that showcases your services. Utilize social media, email marketing and paid advertising to reach potential clients.

Step 7: Build a network
Connect with other web developers, designers and entrepreneurs in your niche. Join online communities, attend conferences and participate in web development forums to build your network.

Step 8: Offer exceptional customer service
Building a successful web development firm requires first-rate customer service. Be sure to communicate effectively and professionally, and to be aware of your clients' needs.

Examples of online platforms for web developers:

Upwork: Upwork is a freelancing platform that connects businesses with web developers from around the world. It's an excellent platform for building your portfolio and finding clients.

Fiverr: Fiverr is a platform that allows web developers to offer their services to clients worldwide. You can set your prices and build a reputation based on the quality of your work.

Freelancer: Freelancer is another freelancing platform that connects businesses with web developers, designers and other professionals. You can bid on projects and build your reputation through positive client feedback.

Toptal: Toptal is a platform that connects businesses with top web developers, designers and project managers. Toptal requires that developers undergo a rigorous screening process to ensure that only the best are accepted.

Codeable: Codeable is a platform that specializes in WordPress development. It connects businesses with WordPress developers who are vetted and experienced in building custom WordPress solutions.

In conclusion, starting a web development business online requires dedication, a strong skill set and a solid business plan. With the right approach, you can build a successful web development business that provides value to clients and fulfills your entrepreneurial ambitions.

For people who enjoy writing, editing, and assisting others in achieving their career goals, starting an online resume writing service may be a lucrative and rewarding endeavor. The following steps will show you how to launch an online resume writing business:

Step 1: Determine your target market

You need to decide who your ideal clients are. Are you targeting students, recent graduates, mid-level professionals, executives or people looking for a career change? Knowing your target audience will help you create effective marketing strategies.

Step 2: Develop your services

Decide on the services you will offer. Will you write resumes, cover letters, LinkedIn profiles or provide interview coaching? Consider what sets you apart from other resume writers, such as specialized expertise, certifications or personalized attention to each client.

Step 3: Build your website

A website is crucial for any online business. You can create your website using website builders like Wix, Squarespace or WordPress. Make sure your website is professional-looking and easy to navigate. Include information about your services, pricing, testimonials and a contact form.

Step 4: Create a pricing structure

You need to decide how much you will charge for your services. You can charge per project, per hour or offer packages. Research your competition to ensure your prices are competitive and fair.

Step 5: Develop a marketing strategy

To attract clients, you need to promote your services. Use social media platforms like LinkedIn, Twitter and Facebook to reach out to potential clients. Consider running Google ads, writing blog posts and participating in forums and groups related to your target audience. Building relationships with recruiters, career coaches and HR professionals can also be beneficial.

Step 6: Invest in necessary tools

You will need a computer, internet connection and word processing software. You may also want to invest in design software like Canva or Adobe Creative Suite to create visually appealing resumes and graphics.

Step 7: Develop a process

Establish a workflow that works for you and your clients. Develop a process for gathering information from clients, writing resumes, editing and delivering final products.

Examples of online resume writing businesses:

Resume Writing Group: Resume Writing Group provides professional resume writing services, cover letters and LinkedIn profile writing. They offer a variety of packages to suit different budgets and needs.

TopResume: TopResume is one of the largest resume writing services in the world. They offer resume writing, LinkedIn profile writing and CV writing services.

CraftResumes: CraftResumes is a resume writing service that offers affordable resume writing, cover letter writing and LinkedIn profile writing services.

Resumeble: Resumeble provides professional resume writing services and offers a satisfaction guarantee to their clients. They also offer cover letter and LinkedIn profile writing services.

ResumeSpice: ResumeSpice is a resume writing and career coaching service that offers resume writing, LinkedIn profile writing and interview coaching services. They also offer a 60-day interview guarantee to their clients.

In conclusion, starting an online resume writing business requires careful planning and a clear understanding of your target audience, services, pricing, marketing strategy and necessary tools. By following these steps, you can create a successful and profitable business that helps others achieve their career goals. Remember to establish a solid workflow that works for you and your clients and always strive to provide personalized and high quality services to stand out in a competitive market.

Your search engine optimization abilities can be profitablely used in an online SEO consultancy firm. Here are some starting points:

Step 1: Develop your SEO skills

You must have a thorough understanding of search engine optimization to launch an SEO consulting service. Analyze websites and identify areas for improvement. Consider taking online courses or reading books on the subject.

Step 2: Define your target market

The kind of clients you want to work with should be defined. Are you targeting small businesses or large corporations? Focus on a specific industry to help develop your marketing strategy.

Step 3: Create a website

A website is essential for any online business, including an SEO consulting business. Showcase your skills and expertise in SEO, provide information about your services and pricing. Use website builders like Wix, Squarespace, or WordPress to create your website.

Step 4: Develop a marketing strategy

Use online advertising, social media, email marketing, and networking to promote your business. Consider offering a free SEO audit or consultation to attract potential clients.

Step 5: Set your pricing

Decide how you want to charge for your services. You can charge hourly rates or offer packages that include a set number of hours or specific services. Research what other SEO consultants are charging to ensure competitive pricing.

Step 6: Deliver high quality work

To keep clients coming back and referring others to your business, deliver high quality work. Stay up-to-date with the latest SEO techniques and strategies, communicate regularly with your clients to ensure you are meeting their needs.

Some examples of successful SEO consulting businesses include:

Moz offers a range of SEO tools and resources, as well as consulting services. Their website provides lots of valuable SEO information and they have a blog and community forum where SEO professionals can share their knowledge and expertise.

Backlinko is an SEO blog run by Brian Dean, who is known for his expertise in link building. Backlinko offers a range of SEO courses and consulting services.

Neil Patel Digital provides SEO consulting services, as well as digital marketing and website design services. Neil Patel is a well-known digital marketing expert who has worked with a range of large companies.

The HOTH is an SEO company that offers a range of services, including consulting, link building and content creation. They have worked with thousands of businesses and have a team of experienced SEO professionals.

Search Engine Land is a leading industry source for daily, must-read news and in-depth analysis about search engine optimization and marketing. They provide updates on SEO best practices, algorithm changes, and insights, making it a go-to resource for both new and seasoned SEO professionals.

Starting an online SEO consulting business can be a great way to turn your passion for search engine optimization into a profitable business. Follow these steps and learn from successful SEO consultants to build a thriving business and help other businesses improve their search engine rankings.

Starting an internet transcription company might be a terrific way to work from home or start a side business. To get started, go to the following step-by-step instructions:

Step 1: Research the market
Determine the demand for transcription services in your target market. Look for potential clients, such as podcasters, content creators or small businesses. Also, check out the competition and analyze their pricing and services.

Step 2: Choose a niche
Consider specializing in a specific industry or type of transcription, such as legal or medical transcription. Specializing can help you stand out in the market and increase your rates.

Step 3: Get the necessary equipment
To start an online transcription business, you'll need a computer, a reliable internet connection, transcription software, headphones and a foot pedal. You can find these tools on various online platforms.

Step 4: Develop your skills
Improve your typing speed and accuracy by practicing transcription exercises. Also, consider taking online courses or certifications to learn more about the transcription industry.

Step 5: Set your rates
Determine your pricing based on your level of experience, the complexity of the job and the market's standards. You can charge per audio minute or per hour.

Step 6: Build your online presence
Create a website and social media accounts to showcase your services, expertise and portfolio. Also, use SEO techniques to optimize your website and attract potential clients.

Step 7: Find clients
Reach out to potential clients, such as content creators or small businesses and offer your services. You can also use online platforms, such as Upwork or Fiverr, to find clients.

Step 8: Deliver high quality work
Make sure to deliver accurate and timely transcripts to your clients. Use software to proofread your work and ensure its quality.

Examples of online transcription businesses include:

Transcription Hub - an online platform that offers transcription services for various industries, including legal, medical and academic.

SpeakWrite - a leading transcription service provider that caters to various industries, such as law enforcement, legal, and government sectors, offering fast and accurate transcription services.

Rev - an online platform that provides transcription, captioning and subtitling services for businesses, individuals and organizations.

Scribie - an affordable online transcription company that provides transcription services to diverse industries.

GoTranscript - an online platform that provides transcription services for businesses, podcasts and content creators.

In conclusion, starting an online transcription business can provide a flexible and lucrative career opportunity for those with strong typing skills and attention to detail. By following the steps outlined above, including researching the market, developing your skills and building your online presence, you can establish yourself as a successful transcription professional. Don't forget to deliver high quality work and maintain positive relationships with your clients to ensure ongoing success.

If you're good at noticing small mistakes and enjoy reading and writing, you can start a business checking other people's writing online. Lots of businesses need people to check their work, like publishers, marketers, and teachers. There are more and more jobs for people who can check and correct writing. Here are the steps to start your own proofreading business online.

Step 1: Choose Your Specialty
Decide what kind of proofreading you want to do before starting your online proofreading business. You can specialize in academic, legal, medical, technical, or general proofreading. This will help you to target your audience and make your business stand out.

Step 2: Improve Your Skills
To become a successful proofreader, you need to be great at spelling, punctuation, and grammar. You also need to be detail-oriented and efficient. Consider taking online courses or attending workshops to improve your skills and keep up with industry trends.

Step 3: Start Your Business
After developing your skills, it's time to set up your online proofreading business. This involves selecting a business name, registering your business, building a website, and setting up a payment system.

Step 4: Create a Portfolio
To attract customers, you need to create a strong portfolio that showcases your skills and experience. Offer proofreading services to friends and family and ask for their feedback and testimonials.

Step 5: Advertise Your Services
Marketing is important for any business, and your online proofreading business is no different. Use social media, email marketing, and online ads to reach potential customers. Join online groups and forums related to your specialty to network with other professionals and learn about job opportunities.

Step 6: Decide Your Prices
Decide on your prices based on your experience and industry standards. Offer different pricing options to fit the needs and budgets of your clients.

Step 7: Provide Great Customer Service
Providing excellent customer service is crucial to building a strong reputation and keeping clients. Respond quickly to customer inquiries and deliver high quality work on time.

Here are some successful online proofreading businesses that can serve as inspiration:

ProofreadingPal: This online proofreading service provides editing and proofreading services for businesses, students and authors. They have been in business since 2010 and have a team of experienced proofreaders.

EditFast: EditFast is an online editing and proofreading service that connects clients with freelance editors and proofreaders. They have been in business since 1998 and have worked with clients such as Microsoft and IBM.

Polished Paper: Polished Paper offers editing and proofreading services for academic, business and personal documents. They have a team of professional editors and offer a satisfaction guarantee.

Grammarly: Grammarly is a widely-used online writing assistant that not only offers grammar checking but also style and tone suggestions. While it automates the proofreading process, it's an essential tool for many writers, students, and professionals looking to polish their documents.

Scribendi: Scribendi is an international editing and proofreading company in operation since 1997. They offer services ranging from academic paper editing to book editing and have a large team of professional editors.

Starting an online proofreading business requires excellent writing and grammar skills, attention to detail, and strong marketing skills. By following these steps and staying committed to your business, you can build a successful online proofreading business and help clients improve the quality of their written content.

If you love writing and understand marketing, you can make money by starting your own online copywriting business. Here are the steps to get started:

Step 1: Improve your writing skills

As a copywriter, you should have good writing and communication skills. You can take courses or workshops to improve your grammar, punctuation and language usage.

Step 2: Choose your specialty

There are different types of copywriting, such as SEO copywriting, email marketing, sales copy and content marketing. Pick a niche that interests you and that you are passionate about.

Step 3: Create your portfolio

To attract clients, you need to show your skills and abilities. Start by writing sample pieces that showcase your skills in your chosen specialty.

Step 4: Make your website

Having a professional website is important for an online business. You can use website builders like Wix, Squarespace or WordPress to create your site. Make sure it is easy to navigate, user-friendly and showcases your portfolio.

Step 5: Set your rates

Research what other copywriters in your niche charge and set your rates accordingly. You can offer discounts for bulk orders or package deals.

Step 6: Promote your services

Start promoting your services on social media, blogs and forums related to your niche. Network with other professionals in the industry and offer to provide guest posts and content for their websites.

Step 7: Provide excellent work

Your reputation is important in the copywriting industry. Make sure you deliver high quality work on time and exceed your clients' expectations. This will help you build a strong client base and receive positive referrals.

Some examples of successful online copywriting businesses include:

Copify, a UK-based online copywriting agency that delivers high-quality content solutions to businesses of all sizes.

Express Writers, a United States-based agency renowned for its diverse copywriting services, including blog writing, email marketing, and social media content creation.

The Creative Copywriter, a UK-based agency with a distinctive specialization in crafting compelling copy for creative industry businesses.

Smartblogger, a prominent online platform providing an array of invaluable resources and educational courses to empower aspiring copywriters in honing their craft.

ProBlogger, a trusted source offering a wide range of resources, as well as job listings, catering to the needs of freelance writers and bloggers.

In summary, starting an online copywriting business can be a profitable career if you have the skills and passion for it. Follow these steps to establish a successful online copywriting business and gain a good reputation in the industry. Remember to work hard, stay committed and always strive for excellence to achieve long-term success.

You need to pay close attention to detail, have strong grammar and spelling abilities, and have editing and proofreading experience in order to start an internet editing business. To start an internet editing business, you should do the following:

Step 1: Determine your niche
Consider what type of editing services you want to provide, such as academic, business, creative writing or technical editing.

Step 2: Develop your skills
To become an editor, you should, of course have excellent language skills. You can take courses or certifications in editing and proofreading to improve your skills.

Step 3: Set your prices
Research your competitors' rates and determine a pricing strategy that works for you.

Step 4: Create a website
Create a professional website that showcases your services, rates and testimonials from satisfied clients. You can use website builders like Wix or WordPress to create your website.

Step 5: Develop a marketing strategy
Promote your services on social media, like LinkedIn and Twitter. Also running email marketing campaigns.

Step 6: Set up payment options
Set up payment options for your clients, such as PayPal or Stripe and create an invoice template to send to your clients.

Step 7: Build your network
Connect with potential clients and other editors in your niche. You can join online communities like Editors Association of Earth or Freelance Editors Network to find work opportunities and connect with other editors.

Examples of online editing businesses:

EditMyEnglish provides editing services to ESL students and professionals.

Scribendi provides proofreading and editing services for businesses, academics and authors.

Grammar Chic offers editing and writing services for individuals and businesses.

ProofreadingPal offers proofreading and editing services for a variety of documents, including academic papers, business documents and personal documents.

Polished Paper provides proofreading and editing services for businesses, academics and authors.

In conclusion, starting an online editing business can be a fulfilling and profitable venture, especially for those with a keen eye for detail and a passion for language. By following the steps outlined above, you can develop the skills necessary to become an expert editor, determine your niche, set your pricing strategy, create a professional website, and promote your services through targeted marketing campaigns. As you build your network and gain experience, you can expand your business, increase your rates and establish yourself as a leader in your field. With hard work and dedication, starting an online editing business can be a great way to turn your passion for language into a successful career.

You might wish to create an online travel agency if you are interested in the travel business. The following section outlines the steps for starting an online travel agency:

Step 1: Research and Identify your niche
Before starting an online travel booking business, it is important to research and identify your target market. You may decide to specialize in luxury travel, adventure travel or budget travel.

Step 2: Choose a name for your firm.
Make sure the name you choose is memorable and catchy. The simplest way to determine this is to just see if the name is accessible as a domain name.

Step 3: Register your business
Register your business as a sole proprietorship, LLC or corporation. For guidance on the optimal business structure for your requirements, speak with an accountant or a lawyer.

Step 4: Create a website
Create a professional-looking website. One that is user-friendly and easy to navigate. Make sure that it is optimized for search engines and mobile devices.

Step 5: Partner with travel agencies and airlines
Partner with travel agencies and airlines to offer your customers a variety of travel options. Consider partnering with hotels and car rental companies as well.

Step 6: Set up payment systems
Set up payment systems such as PayPal or Stripe to process payments from your customers. Ensure that your website is secure and protected from hackers.

Step 7: Promote your business
Promote your online travel booking business through social media, Google Ads and other advertising platforms. Consider offering discounts and incentives to attract customers.

Examples of Online Travel Booking Businesses:

Expedia.com: Expedia is a travel booking website that offers a wide range of travel options such as flights, hotels, car rentals and vacation packages.

Booking.com: Booking.com is another popular online travel booking platform that allows customers to book hotels, apartments, resorts and villas.

Airbnb: Airbnb is a popular online travel booking platform that connects travelers with hosts who rent out their homes, apartments or rooms.

Travelocity: Travelocity is an online travel booking platform that allows customers to book flights, hotels, car rentals and vacation packages.

Kayak.com: Kayak is a travel search engine that helps customers find the best travel deals by searching multiple travel websites at once.

In conclusion, starting an online travel booking business can be a profitable venture with the right steps. Identify your niche, choose a memorable name, register your business, create a professional website, partner with travel agencies and airlines, set up payment systems and promote your business through advertising and incentives. Remember to prioritize customer satisfaction and stay up-to-date with industry trends for continued success.

Starting an online event planning company can be a fun and rewarding way to work from home. Here are some guidelines to get you started:

Step 1: Determine your niche
You need to decide on the type of events you want to plan. It could be weddings, corporate events, conferences or parties. You can choose to specialize in a particular niche or be a general event planner.

Step 2: Create a business plan
Once you have determined your niche, you need to create a business plan that outlines your goals, target audience, services, pricing, marketing strategy and financial projections.

Step 3: Register your business
Choose a business name and register it with the relevant authorities in your country. You may need to obtain a business license, tax identification number and other permits to operate legally.

Step 4: Create a website
Your website is your online storefront and it's where potential clients will go to learn more about your services. Choose a domain name that reflects your business name and create a professional-looking website that showcases your work, services, pricing and testimonials.

Step 5: Set up payment systems
You need to set up payment systems that allow your clients to pay for your services easily. Consider using payment gateways like PayPal, Stripe or Square to process payments securely.

Step 6: Promote your business
Once you have everything set up, it's time to start promoting your business. Use social media platforms like Facebook, Instagram, Twitter and LinkedIn to reach out to potential clients. You can also consider running ads on social media or Google AdWords to boost your visibility.

Step 7: Build your network
As an event planner, it's crucial to build relationships with vendors and suppliers. Attend networking events, conferences and exhibitions to connect with other professionals in the industry. You can also join online groups or forums to expand your network.

Examples of online event planning businesses:

Eventique is a global event planning company that caters to both corporate and personal events. Their professional team ensures every detail is taken care of, making every event unique and memorable.

The Event Group is an online event planning company that creates memorable events for businesses and individuals. They offer services like event design, vendor management, venue sourcing and event production.

Bespoke Events crafts exceptional experiences tailored to individual tastes and preferences. With a deep understanding of modern aesthetics and timeless traditions, they offer event planning for weddings, corporate events, and special occasions.

Event Planet is an online event planning company that offers event management services for corporate clients. Their services include event design, budget management, vendor management and event production.

Epic Events is a premier online event planning service specializing in both intimate events and grand gatherings. They pride themselves in creating memorable experiences, ensuring every occasion is epic and unforgettable.

In conclusion, starting an online event planning business can be a fulfilling and lucrative venture that allows you to work from home. By following the steps outlined above, you can establish a successful business that caters to your chosen niche. Remember to create a solid business plan, register your business, build a professional website, set up payment systems, promote your business and network with other professionals in the industry. With determination and hard work, you can turn your passion for event planning into a thriving business.

Buying and selling websites for a profit is the first step in starting a website flipping business online. Here are some guidelines for getting started:

Step 1: Develop your skills
To be successful in website flipping, you need to have a good understanding of web design, online marketing and website analytics. You can take online courses or get certifications to develop your skills.

Step 2: Choose a niche
Focus on a specific niche that you are passionate about or have experience in. This will help you to understand the audience better, the competition and the potential value of the website.

Step 3: Find undervalued websites
Use websites like Flippa, Empire Flippers and WebsiteBroker to find undervalued websites that you can buy for a low price. Look for websites with high traffic, good SEO and a solid revenue stream.

Step 4: Evaluate the website
Conduct thorough due diligence to evaluate the website's revenue, traffic and potential. You can use tools like Ahrefs, SEMrush and Google Analytics to analyze the website's performance.

Step 5: Make improvements
Once you have acquired the website, make improvements to increase its value. This may include optimizing the website's SEO, improving the website design and increasing traffic.

Step 6: Sell the website
After making the necessary improvements, you can list the website for sale on the same platforms where you found it. It's essential to emphasize the site's enhancements and potential for growth to entice potential buyers.

Examples of successful website flipping businesses include:

Flippa: Flippa is one of the most popular online marketplaces for buying and selling websites, domains, and mobile apps. They have facilitated a large number of transactions and have a wide range of listings, from starter sites to well-established online businesses.

Empire Flippers: Empire Flippers is a marketplace for buying and selling online businesses. They provide a platform that lists vetted online businesses for potential investors and have facilitated millions of dollars in transactions over the years.

Quiet Light Brokerage: Quiet Light Brokerage is a website brokerage that specializes in selling established online businesses. The platform has sold over $100 million worth of online businesses since its inception in 2007.

FE International: FE International is a leading M&A advisor for SaaS, e-commerce, and content businesses. With a proven track record of successful transactions, they provide a full brokerage service for online business owners looking to sell or acquire digital assets.

WebsiteProperties: WebsiteProperties is a full-service website brokerage specializing in selling internet-based businesses. With their experience and expertise, they help clients prepare, appraise, market, and sell their online businesses.

Starting an online website flipping business can be a lucrative and rewarding venture. With the right skills and strategy, you can buy and sell websites for a profit and build a successful business.

If you have a great voice and love voice acting, you can start an online voice over business and earn money. Here are the steps to get started:

Step 1: Get the right equipment

To start your online voice over business, you need a good microphone, a computer with audio editing software, and a quiet place to record.

Step 2: Improve your skills

To be a great voice actor, you need to practice regularly. Take voice acting classes or workshops, watch YouTube tutorials, and practice different styles like commercials, narration, and character acting.

Step 3: Create a portfolio

Your portfolio showcases your work and helps you get clients. Record sample voice overs of different styles and offer your services for free to build your portfolio.

Step 4: Build a website

Your website will help you establish an online presence. Include your portfolio, services, and a way for potential clients to contact you.

Step 5: Find clients

Use online platforms like Upwork, Fiverr, and Freelancer.com to find voice over work. Reach out to companies that produce commercials, audiobooks, and e-learning materials too.

Step 6: Promote your services

Use social media platforms like Twitter and Instagram to showcase your work and connect with potential clients. Create a demo reel, attend networking events, and collaborate with other voice actors to promote your services.

Examples of successful online voice over businesses include:

Joe Zieja Voice Acting: Joe Zieja is a successful voice actor who has worked on video games, anime, and commercials. His website showcases his portfolio and services, and he also offers coaching services to help other voice actors improve their skills.

Voice123: Voice123 is a leading online platform where voice actors can create a profile and find work. Clients can post job opportunities, and voice actors can submit auditions directly on the platform. It is renowned for its professional and broad range of voice talents.

Voices.com: Voices.com is a popular online platform where clients can search for and hire voice actors for a variety of projects, including commercials, animation, and video games. Voice actors can create a profile and apply for job opportunities directly on the platform.

Bill DeWees Voice Over: Bill DeWees is a seasoned voice over artist known for his work in commercials, corporate videos, e-learning, and audiobooks. His website not only highlights his extensive portfolio but also offers training programs, tutorials, and resources for aspiring voice-over professionals to build their careers.

Overall, starting a voice over business online requires a combination of skill, equipment and marketing. With dedication and hard work, it is possible to build a successful voice over business and make a living doing what you love.

To start an online legal consulting business and offer top-notch legal services to your clients, you'll need to take a few important steps. Follow these steps to get started:

Step 1: Choose your focus
Make sure you have the necessary training and expertise for the legal field that most interests you, such as business or family law.

Step 2: Set up your business
Pick a business name and register it with your local government. Get any permits or licenses you need to run a legal consulting business in your area.

Step 3: Create a website
Your website is how clients will find you. Make sure it looks professional and has all the information they need. Put your qualifications, prices and contact details on there.

Step 4: Decide on pricing
Look up what other legal consultants in your area are charging and decide on your own prices. Consider offering a discount for first-time clients.

Step 5: Advertise your business
Use social media, paid ads and other marketing methods to get the word out about your business. Email potential clients and go to events to meet new people.

Step 6: Keep clients happy
Stay in touch with your clients and make sure they're happy with your services. Offer additional help if they need it.

Examples of websites where you can start your online legal consulting business include:

LegalZoom - LegalZoom is an online platform that provides legal services such as business formation, contracts and trademark registration.

Avvo - Avvo is a website that offers legal advice and connects clients with lawyers who can help with their legal issues.

Rocket Lawyer - Rocket Lawyer is an online platform that provides legal services, including legal documents and consultations with lawyers.

UpCounsel - UpCounsel is a website that connects businesses with on-demand lawyers who can provide legal advice and services.

Starting an online legal consulting business takes careful planning. To provide good legal services to clients, you must choose your specialty, create a website, set your prices, market your business well, and keep in touch with clients. By doing these things, you can build a successful online legal consulting business that attracts clients and gives them the help they need.

You may convert your love of design into a successful company by starting an online interior design firm. The following are the steps to start:

Step 1: Determine your niche
Decide on the specific area of interior design you want to focus on such as residential, commercial or sustainable design.

Step 2: Develop a portfolio
Create a portfolio showcasing your design work to potential clients. This can include before and after photos, design plans and client testimonials.

Step 3: Set pricing and services
Determine your pricing structure and services you will offer such as consultation, design planning and project management.

Step 4: Choose a business name and create a website
Choose a name that represents your brand and create a professional website showcasing your portfolio and services.

Step 5: Market your business
Use social media, search engine optimization and online advertising to promote your business and reach potential clients.

Step 6: Set up a virtual design process
Establish a process for virtual consultations, design planning and communication with clients.

Step 7: Collaborate with contractors and vendors
Build relationships with contractors and vendors to facilitate the implementation of your design plans.

Some platforms where you can start your online interior design business include:

Houzz Pro: A platform that offers project management, 3D visualization, and client communication tools for interior designers and decorators.

DesignFiles: A comprehensive online platform catering to interior designers that provides tools for mood board creation, product sourcing, and client communication, making the design process smoother.

Havenly: A platform that provides virtual interior design services to clients, catering to both residential and commercial projects.

RoomSketcher: RoomSketcher provides interactive floor plans and home design tools that allow interior designers to create 2D and 3D visualizations, which can be shared with clients for a more immersive design experience.

eDesign Tribe is a community and platform tailored for eDesign professionals. It offers resources, courses, and a space for designers to showcase their work and connect with potential clients. The platform also provides tools tailored specifically for the virtual interior design process.

Starting an online interior design business may take some time and effort, but with a solid portfolio and marketing strategy, it can be a fulfilling and profitable venture.

Planning and carrying out a start-up for an online customer service firm demands caution. You can start by following the steps listed below:

Step 1: Identify your niche

Decide on the type of customer service business you want to offer. It could be email support, chat support, social media management or phone support.

Step 2: Research your market

Find out who your target audience is and what they need in terms of customer service. Look at what your competitors are doing and how they are pricing their services.

Step 3: Choose your business model

Decide whether you want to offer your services as a freelancer or set up a virtual call center. If you're working alone, you can start as a freelancer and later build a team as your business grows.

Step 4: Create a business plan

Write down your business goals, marketing strategies, pricing and operational procedures. This will help you stay focused and organized.

Step 5: Set up your business

Register your business, set up a website and create social media profiles. Choose a name that's catchy and easy to remember.

Step 6: Invest in the right tools

You'll need a reliable computer, a high-speed internet connection, a good headset and customer service software like Zendesk or Help Scout.

Step 7: Market your business

Reach out to potential clients via email, social media or other online platforms. Create a portfolio of your work and showcase your expertise. Offer free consultations or trials to attract new clients.

Step 8: Provide excellent customer service

Deliver high quality services and exceed your clients' expectations. Build lasting relationships with your clients and encourage them to refer you to others.

Some examples of online customer service businesses are:

Fancy Hands: A virtual assistant service that provides email and phone support, appointment scheduling and research services.

24/7 Virtual Assistant: A virtual assistant service that offers a range of customer service solutions, including chat and email support, social media management and phone support.

Arise: A virtual call center that allows you to work from home and provide customer service support to clients in various industries.

Smith.ai: A company known for its virtual receptionist and client engagement services, providing phone support, appointment scheduling, and lead qualification.

Support Ninja: A virtual customer support company that offers email, chat and phone support, as well as social media management and customer engagement services.

Starting an online customer service business can be profitable if you approach it strategically. To start, identify your niche and research your market. Choose a business model and create a business plan with a catchy name. Invest in the right tools and market your business to attract clients. Provide excellent customer service to ensure clients receive high quality services. Build lasting relationships with clients to encourage referrals and grow your business.

You can use these easy procedures to sell your images online if you're an excellent photographer and want to earn some money:

Step 1: Determine your niche
Make a choice regarding the types of pictures you want to sell. Photography of events, nature, or any other subject matter is possible. Focusing on your target market will be made easier thanks to this.

Step 2: Build your portfolio
Make a collection of your finest photos to display on your website. To attract the interest of potential buyers, make sure they are of high quality and appealing to the eye.

Step 3: Choose a platform
Select a platform where you can sell your photos online. Some popular options are Shutterstock, iStock, and Adobe Stock. You can upload your images to these platforms, and you'll earn a commission every time someone buys one of your photos.

Step 4: Create a website
Consider building your own website to sell your photos directly to customers. By doing this, you'll have more control over your pricing and branding. You don't need any coding skills to create a professional-looking website. You can use website builders like Wix, Squarespace, or WordPress to help you.

Step 5: Set your prices
Determine how much you want to charge for your photos. Research the market to see what other photographers are charging for similar images. Keep in mind that pricing too high or too low can affect your sales.

Step 6: Promote your business
Start promoting your business through social media, email marketing, and other channels to attract customers. Consider offering discounts or special promotions to incentivize sales. You can also collaborate with other photographers or blogs to increase your exposure.

Examples of successful online photo selling businesses include:

Peter McKinnon: Peter is a popular YouTuber and photographer who sells his images on his website. He offers a variety of prints, canvases and other products featuring his photos.

Alex Strohl: Alex is a travel photographer who sells his images through Adobe Stock. He also offers workshops and photography courses through his website.

Rachel Gulotta and Daniel Inskeep: Rachel and Daniel are photographers who run Mango Street, a website that offers courses, tutorials and presets for other photographers. They also sell their own images and prints on their website.

Thomas Heaton: Thomas is a landscape photographer who documents his journeys on YouTube. He offers prints of his scenic captures through his official website.

Elia Locardi: Elia is known for his travel and landscape photography. He sells prints of his stunning shots on his website and also offers in-depth photography tutorials.

The process of starting an internet photo-selling business is difficult and time-consuming. You may, however, make your passion for taking pictures into a successful business provided you are committed to making it happen and have a solid plan in place. Just keep in mind that building a successful company requires time and work; success doesn't happen quickly. You may accomplish your objectives and live out your aspirations of becoming a successful online photo seller.

A great way to turn your love of fashion into a lucrative business is to launch an online fashion retailer. The following are the steps to start:

Step 1: Identify your niche
Choose the fashion products you want to sell online first. Women's clothing, men's clothing, kids' clothing, shoes, accessories, or a combination of these can fall under this category.

Step 2: Choose a business name and register it
Choose a distinctive company name, then register it with your state's government. You might also need to register for sales tax and obtain a tax ID number.

Step 3: Develop a business plan
Make a business plan that includes an overview of your goals, target market, marketing plans, financial projections, and other important details.

Step 4: Set up your website
Create an online store using a platform for online shopping such as Shopify, WooCommerce, or BigCommerce. You can also sell your goods through online stores like Amazon, eBay, or Etsy.

Step 5: Source your products
Find trustworthy manufacturers or distributors for your goods by contacting them directly or using wholesale marketplaces like Alibaba.

Step 6: Create your product listings
Create engaging product descriptions and take professional product photos to display them on your website.

Step 7: Promote your business
Showcase your products on social media sites like Instagram, Facebook, and Twitter and interact with your target market. On these platforms, you can also run paid advertising campaigns to reach a larger audience.

To keep your customers satisfied and coming back for more, make sure that orders are fulfilled promptly and offer top-notch customer service.

Examples of leading online fashion selling businesses:

Fashion Nova is an American-based online fashion retailer that specializes in trendy clothing for women. They are known for their affordable and fashionable clothes and have gained a significant social media following due to their influencer marketing strategy.

ASOS is a UK-based online fashion and beauty store that offers clothing, accessories and beauty products for men and women. They have a global presence and a wide range of products, catering to various fashion styles and budgets.

Boohoo is a UK-based online fashion retailer that offers affordable fashion for women and men. They have a fast fashion business model and are known for their trendy designs and frequent sales.

Missguided is a UK-based online fashion retailer that offers fast fashion for women. They have a focus on trendy designs and affordable prices and have a strong presence on social media platforms.

PrettyLittleThing is a UK-based online fashion retailer that offers trendy clothing and accessories for women. They have a fast fashion business model and are known for their collaboration with celebrities and influencers.

In conclusion, launching an online fashion business requires careful planning, original thought, as well as effective execution. You can make your love of fashion into a successful business by following the above-mentioned steps.

You may convert your love of crafts into a successful company by starting an online craft selling website. A step-by-step tutorial for getting started is provided below:

Step 1: Decide on the type of crafts you want to sell
You need to determine what kind of crafts you want to sell, whether it's jewelry, home decor items, artwork, or any other craft.

Step 2: Determine your target market
It's essential to identify your target market to determine your pricing strategy, marketing strategy and the type of crafts you should be making.

Step 3: Create a brand name and logo
Choose a catchy name that is easy to remember and create a logo that reflects your brand's personality.

Step 4: Build an online store
You can create an online store using platforms such as Etsy, Shopify, Amazon Handmade or Big Cartel. These platforms provide easy-to-use templates, tools and resources to build an online store with no coding or design experience.

Step 5: Create quality product listings
Create high quality product listings with detailed descriptions, high quality images and a pricing strategy that will attract customers.

Step 6: Market your products
Use social media platforms like Facebook, Instagram, Twitter and Pinterest to promote your products. You can also join relevant groups and forums to promote your crafts.

Step 7: Build a customer base
Offer excellent customer service and ensure your customers are satisfied with their purchases. Encourage your customers to leave reviews and feedback.

Step 8: Evaluate your business
Monitor your sales, expenses and profit margins regularly. Use this data to determine what is working and what isn't and make necessary adjustments to your business strategy.

Examples of successful online craft selling businesses include:

The Handmade Home: This online store sells unique, handmade home decor items that are customized to meet their customers' needs.

Two Wild Hares: This online store specializes in supplies for making bath bombs, soaps, and other handcrafted bath and body products.

The Sewing Loft: This online store sells fabric and sewing patterns, along with tutorials and tips for sewing enthusiasts.

Lemonade Couture: This online store specializes in handmade baby clothes and accessories.

The Little Market: This online marketplace offers a curated selection of handmade goods from artisans all over the world, with a focus on ethical and fair trade products.

In conclusion, starting an online craft selling business can be a profitable venture that allows you to turn your passion for crafts into a thriving business. By identifying your niche, determining your target market, creating a brand name and logo, building an online store, creating quality product listings, marketing your products, building a customer base and evaluating your business regularly, you can increase your chances of success. Remember to provide excellent customer service and adjust your business strategy as needed to stay competitive in the market. With dedication, hard work and a little bit of creativity, you can grow your online craft business and achieve your entrepreneurial goals.

Starting an online art selling business can be an exciting venture for artists who want to sell their creations to a global audience. The following is a guide for starting an online art selling business:

Step 1: Define your niche and target audience

Decide on your target market and unique selling proposition. Do you have a preferred style, medium, or subject? Identify which customer segments to target.

Step 2: Create a portfolio of your artwork

You need to have a portfolio of high quality images of your artwork to showcase on your website. Ensure that the images are clear and the colors are true to life.

Step 3: Choose a platform to sell your artwork

There are several platforms to choose from, including:• Online marketplaces such as Etsy, ArtFire and Redbubble• Dedicated art-selling platforms such as Saatchi Art, Artfinder and Artsy• Building your own e-commerce website using platforms such as Shopify, WooCommerce or Squarespace.

Step 4: Set up your online store

You must set up your online store after choosing your preferred platform. Make sure to include high quality pictures, artwork descriptions, prices, and shipping information.

Step 5: Market your artwork

Once your online store is set up, it's time to start promoting your artwork. Utilize social media platforms, art forums and online communities to reach potential customers. You may also consider running paid advertising campaigns to boost your visibility.

Fulfill orders and manage customer relationships: Once you start receiving orders, ensure that you fulfill them promptly and deliver the artwork safely. It's essential to communicate with your customers throughout the process, answer any questions they may have and provide excellent customer service.

Examples of successful online art selling businesses:

Saatchi Art is an online platform that allows artists to sell their work directly to buyers around the world. The site features a wide range of artwork from emerging and established artists and provides a curated selection of pieces for collectors to choose from.

Artfinder is another popular online marketplace for artists to sell their work. The site has a strong focus on promoting emerging talent and allows artists to keep 70% of the sale price of their artwork.

Artsy is a platform that connects art collectors with galleries and artists from around the world. The site features a wide range of art, including paintings, sculptures and photography and provides a range of tools to help collectors discover new artists and build their collections.

Etsy is an e-commerce website that allows artists to sell handmade and vintage items, including art and photography. The site provides a range of tools for artists to build their own online stores and allows them to set their own prices and shipping policies.

Redbubble is a global online marketplace that allows independent artists to upload and sell their artwork on a variety of products, from prints to clothing to home decor. The platform provides artists the flexibility to set their own margins while ensuring the production, shipping, and customer service aspects are handled by Redbubble itself.

For artists looking to reach a larger audience, starting an online art business can be great. You can build a profitable online art business that appeals to your target market and brings in sales by following these guidelines. Having more control and flexibility by creating your own e-commerce website. Turn your love of art into a successful online business by working hard and with dedication.

Starting an online music selling business requires careful planning, preparation, and attention to detail. By taking the actions described below, you can launch your own online music selling business

Step 1: Research and choose your niche
Consider the genre of music you wish to offer and identify your target audience. You can specialize in a particular genre, artist or era of music.

Step 2: Obtain the necessary licenses
You must first obtain the necessary licenses from the copyright holders or music distributors in order to start selling music online. This will guarantee that you have the authority to market the music you've selected.

Step 3: Create a website
To sell music online, you will need a website that looks professional. You can either hire a web designer to build a website for you or build your own website using a website builder like the ones mentioned later in this book.

Step 4: Create an inventory
Create an inventory of the music you want to sell after obtaining the licenses you need. You can work with artists to offer their music on your platform or you can buy the music directly from distributors.

Step 5: Set up payment and shipping
You must set up a payment gateway making use of services like PayPal, Stripe, or Square in order to accept payments from customers. You must also set up a shipping method in order for your music to be distributed to your audience.

Step 6: Market your business
You must advertise your business to draw in potential clients. You can use social media, email marketing, and other marketing techniques to connect with the relevant audience.

Examples of online music selling businesses:

Bandcamp is a platform that allows musicians to sell their music directly to fans. The site provides tools for artists to create their own custom storefronts, set their own prices and keep a larger percentage of the profits from their sales.

iTunes is an online music store that provides a wide range of music from established artists and up-and-coming musicians. The site allows customers to purchase individual songs or albums and provides a seamless integration with Apple's music streaming service.

Amazon Music is another popular platform that allows users to purchase and stream music. The site provides access to a wide range of music, including exclusive releases and live recordings and offers a range of pricing options to suit different budgets.

Spotify is a music streaming platform that allows users to listen to a wide range of music for free or by subscribing to a premium service. The site provides tools for artists to promote their music and reach new fans and offers a range of features for listeners to discover new music and create their own playlists.

In conclusion, for those with a love of music and an entrepreneurial spirit, starting an online music selling business can be a rewarding endeavor. You can create a profitable online music store and reach a large audience by following these steps. Don't forget to do market research, decide your niche, acquire the required licenses, build an inventory, set up payment and shipping systems, and market your company to draw in clients.

A lucrative approach to monetize your love of photography is to launch an online stock photography business. You can start your own internet stock photography business by taking the following steps:

Step 1: Create a portfolio of high quality images
A portfolio of excellent pictures that you can sell online will be necessary. Take pictures of a wide range of subjects to get started, including people, objects, landscapes, and nature. To include in your portfolio, pick the best images.

Step 2: Choose a niche
Consider specializing in a particular type of photography, such as travel, food or nature. This will help you stand out in a crowded market and attract buyers who are looking for specific types of images.

Step 3: Decide on a pricing model
You have two options for earning revenue from your images. You can charge a fixed price for each image, or you can choose to sell them on a royalty-free basis, meaning that you receive a percentage of each sale whenever someone buys one of your images.

Step 4: Choose an online platform to sell your photos
There are many online platforms that allow you to sell your photos to a global market. Some popular options include Shutterstock, iStock, Getty Images and Adobe Stock. Each platform has its own pricing structure, so do your research to find the one that offers the best rates for your work.

Step 5: Upload your images and start selling
Create an account on the platform you've selected, then upload your images. Make sure to give your images descriptive tags and titles so that customers can find them easily.

Step 6: Promote your business
To sell more, advertise your business on social media and other sites where people like photography. Work with other photographers and companies in your field to help each other get more attention for your work.

Examples of successful online photo selling platforms:

Shutterstock is a global platform that allows you to sell your photos to a wide audience. It offers a flexible pricing structure and a variety of tools to help you promote your work and grow your business.

iStock is a popular platform that offers millions of high quality images to buyers around the world. It offers a simple pricing structure and a range of tools to help you manage your portfolio and promote your work.

Getty Images is a well-established platform that provides access to a vast collection of photos, illustrations and videos. It offers a range of licensing options to suit different needs and budgets and provides a variety of tools to help you manage your portfolio and reach new buyers.

Adobe Stock is an online platform that allows you to sell your photos to millions of customers around the world. It offers a simple pricing structure and a range of tools to help you promote your work and grow your business.

It takes commitment and effort to launch an internet stock photography business, but it can be a satisfying way to turn your love of photography into a successful business.

It can be pretty fun and profitable to run your own podcasting business. If you want to start your own podcast, check out the steps below:

Step 1: Identify Your Niche
Determine what kind of podcast you want to produce and what audience you want to serve. Decide on a theme or topic that you are passionate about and have expertise in.

Step 2: Develop Your Format and Content
Decide on the length and frequency of your podcast episodes. Plan your content and create a backlog of episodes before launching your podcast. Think about how you will engage your audience and what value you will provide to them.

Step 3: Choose Your Equipment
Invest in quality equipment to record your podcast, such as a microphone, headphones and a digital recorder or software. You may also want to consider soundproofing your recording space.

Step 4: Find a Hosting Platform
You will need a hosting platform to store and distribute your podcast episodes. Popular hosting platforms include Buzzsprout, Podbean and Simplecast.

Step 5: Create Cover Art and a Website
Create visually appealing cover art for your podcast and design a website to promote it. Your website can also serve as a platform to offer additional content or sell merchandise related to your podcast.

Step 6: Launch Your Podcast
Submit your podcast to directories such as Apple Podcasts, Spotify and Google Podcasts. Promote your podcast on social media and through word-of-mouth to build your audience.

Examples of successful online podcasting businesses include:

Serial - This podcast became a cultural phenomenon and is widely regarded as one of the most successful podcasts of all time. It tells true crime stories in a serialized format and has won multiple awards for its high quality production and storytelling.

The Joe Rogan Experience - A podcast that features lengthy discussions with guests spanning various fields, including comedians, actors, scientists and politicians. It has amassed over a billion downloads and remains a top podcast worldwide.

How I Built This - This podcast features interviews with successful entrepreneurs and explores the stories behind some of the world's most successful companies. It has a large following and is known for its insightful interviews and inspiring stories.

Stuff You Should Know - Hosted by Josh Clark and Chuck Bryant, this podcast dives into diverse topics, making complex subjects engaging. It's one of the most downloaded podcasts worldwide.

TED Radio Hour - Based on the famous TED Talks, this podcast, hosted by Manoush Zomorodi, delves deeper into groundbreaking ideas and has captivated listeners globally.

Starting an online podcasting business needs hard work and commitment, but it can be worth it. If you make great content, build a group of loyal listeners, and explore ways to earn money, you can turn your love for podcasting into a successful business.

A profitable online video editing business is possible for someone with the right skills and a passion for creating high quality videos. You could follow the steps below:

Step 1: Assess your skills and experience
To start a business in video editing online, you should have experience in video editing and knowledge of software like Adobe Premiere Pro, Final Cut Pro, DaVinci Resolve and others.

Step 2: Identify your target market
Decide who your potential customers are. Think about collaborating with startups, YouTubers, wedding videographers, and anyone else in need of video editing services.

Step 3: Develop a business plan
Create a comprehensive business plan outlining your services, target market, pricing and marketing strategy.

Step 4: Set up your business
Register your business, obtain any necessary licenses and permits and create a professional website that showcases your portfolio, services and contact information.

Step 5: Build your portfolio
Create a portfolio that highlights your top-notch work, highlighting your abilities to cater to clients' requirements.

Step 6: Set your prices
Determine your pricing structure for your services based on industry standards and your level of experience.

Step 7: Create a marketing plan
Make a strategy for bringing in new clients using networking, online advertising, and social media.

Some examples of online video editing businesses are:

MotionCue: A video production company that specializes in animation, explainer videos and marketing videos.

VideoCaddy: Offers a range of video editing services, including color correction, sound editing and visual effects.

Viddedit: An expert video editing company providing post-production services. They offer everything from basic edits to advanced visual effects, catering to both individual and corporate clients.

Animoto: A web-based video creation tool that allows users to create professional-quality videos with customizable templates.

Pond5: An online marketplace for video templates, stock footage, and motion graphics, offering a variety of options for video creators.

In conclusion, starting an online video editing business require both extensive knowledge of the business and skills in video editing. You can begin your online video editing business by identifying your target market, developing a business plan, setting up your business, building your portfolio, establishing your prices, and developing a marketing plan. You can then grow your business by offering more services and reaching out to more customers as you build up knowledge and a satisfied customer base.

TRANSLATE YOUR SKILLS INTO SUCCESS

It can be a terrific approach to help others learn languages to start an online translation teaching business. To get you started, follow these steps:

Step 1: Determine your niche
Decide which language(s) you will teach and which level(s) of proficiency you will focus on. Will you teach beginner, intermediate or advanced students? Will you teach general language skills or specialize in business, medical or legal terminology?

Step 2: Create a curriculum
Develop a course outline and lesson plans based on your niche and target audience. Your curriculum should include a mix of grammar, vocabulary and conversation practice.

Step 3: Choose a platform
Select an online platform for teaching, such as Skype, Zoom or Google Meet. Make sure you have a stable internet connection, a microphone and a camera.

Step 4: Set your rates
Research the market to determine what other online language tutors are charging. Set a competitive rate that reflects your experience and qualifications.

Step 5: Promote your services
Advertise your teaching services on social media platforms, language learning websites and other online forums. Create a website to showcase your credentials and services.

Step 6: Develop teaching materials
Create teaching materials such as worksheets, exercises and flashcards to supplement your lessons. You can also recommend textbooks or other learning resources to your students.

Examples of successful online translation teaching businesses:

iTalki: With over 5 million students and 10,000 teachers, iTalki is a popular platform for connecting language learners with qualified teachers from around the world. The platform offers flexible scheduling and a variety of teaching options, including one-on-one lessons, group classes and conversation partners.

Verbling: Verbling is another popular platform that connects language learners with experienced teachers. The platform offers live classes, self-paced courses and personalized learning plans to help students achieve their language goals. Verbling also provides tools for tracking progress and practicing conversation skills.

Preply: Preply is an online learning platform that offers one-on-one lessons with experienced language tutors. The platform provides a range of tools and resources to help students and teachers connect, including video chat, scheduling tools and a secure payment system.

Babbel: Babbel is a language learning platform that offers both courses and live one-on-one lessons with experienced tutors. Their focus is on conversation skills and real-life scenarios, aiming to get learners speaking confidently in their chosen language as quickly as possible.

In conclusion, starting an online translation teaching business can be a rewarding way to share your language expertise with others. To get started, determine your niche, create a curriculum, choose a platform, set competitive rates, promote your services and develop teaching materials. Consider successful platforms like iTalki, Verbling and Preply as examples of what's possible in this industry. With the right approach and dedication, you can create a successful online translation teaching business and make a positive impact on your students' language learning journey.

Starting an online consulting business is a fantastic opportunity to work for yourself and help others manage their finances. To get started, follow these steps:

Step 1: Determine your niche
Consider what area of financial consulting you want to focus on. Do you want to specialize in personal finance, business finance, taxes, investments or something else? Identifying your niche will help you better target your services to your audience.

Step 2: Get certified
While not always necessary, obtaining certification or licensing in your area of financial consulting can help establish credibility with potential clients. Some common certifications in the financial consulting industry include Certified Financial Planner (CFP), Chartered Financial Analyst (CFA) and Certified Public Accountant (CPA).

Step 3: Build your website
Your website will serve as your online storefront, so it's important to invest time and effort in creating a professional-looking and informative website. Include information about your services, rates, certifications and experience. Consider including a blog section where you can provide helpful financial tips and advice to potential clients.

Step 4: Set your rates
Determine how much you will charge for your services. Consider factors such as your level of experience, your certifications and the complexity of the work you will be doing. Be sure to research your competition to ensure your rates are competitive.

Step 5: Build your network
Use social media platforms like LinkedIn to connect with potential clients and other financial professionals in your industry. Attend networking events and conferences to build your network and establish yourself as an expert in your field.

Examples of online financial consulting businesses include:

LearnLux: An online financial wellness platform that offers personalized financial coaching and educational resources to individuals and businesses.

Facet Wealth: A virtual financial planning firm that connects clients with certified financial planners for customized financial advice.

The Financial Gym: A virtual financial coaching service that offers personalized financial plans and guidance to help individuals reach their financial goals.

XY Planning Network: XY Planning Network is an online platform that connects consumers with financial advisors who specialize in serving Gen X and Gen Y clients. Offering a range of services, from investment management to financial planning, the platform aims to make financial advice accessible to younger generations.

Remember, starting an online financial consulting business takes time, effort and dedication. With the right skills and mindset, you can establish yourself as a trusted financial consultant and help people achieve their financial goals.

You may convert your passion for fashion into a successful business by starting an online personal shopping service. To get started, follow the steps below:

Step 1: Identify your target audience
Identify your ideal customers and the products they are most likely to be interested in. Age, gender, style, budget, and location are important factors.

Step 2: Create a business plan
Create a business plan that outlines your goals, ideal customers, pricing strategy, promotional strategies, and projected financial results. As you develop your company, this will assist you in remaining organized and focused.

Step 3: Build your online presence
Set up a website, social media accounts and a blog to showcase your products and services. Use high quality images and engaging content to attract potential customers.

Step 4: Build relationships with suppliers
Research and establish relationships with suppliers that can provide the products you want to sell. Negotiate wholesale pricing and work out any logistical details.

Step 5: Determine your pricing strategy
Decide on your pricing strategy, taking into account your costs, profit margin and market demand. Consider offering free shipping or other promotions to attract customers.

Step 6: Market your business
Use social media, email marketing and other online advertising channels to promote your business and attract new customers. Consider partnering with influencers or offering referral incentives to grow your customer base.

Step 7: Provide excellent customer service
Offer exceptional customer service by responding promptly to inquiries, processing orders quickly and providing personalized shopping experiences.

Examples of successful online personal shopping businesses:

Stitch Fix: Uses a combination of data and personal stylists to curate personalized boxes of clothing and accessories for customers. Customers fill out a style profile and Stitch Fix sends them a box of items tailored to their preferences.

Wantable: A personalized styling service that sends customers clothing or accessories tailored to their preferences. Customers take a style quiz, and a personal stylist curates a collection of items for them. They can try on the items at home, keep what they love, and return what they don't.

Dia & Co: A personal styling service that focuses exclusively on plus-size clothing. Customers complete a style quiz and a personal stylist sends them a box of items tailored to their preferences and size.

Lookiero: An online personal styling service where customers receive a selection of five pieces chosen by a personal stylist based on the customer's preferences. The customer then has the option to keep what they love and return the rest.

In conclusion, for those who have a passion for fashion, starting an online personal shopping business can be exciting and rewarding. You can successfully launch and expand your business by following the above steps. You can build a successful online business out of your love of fashion by putting the right plans in place.

A wonderful method to spread the word about your fitness knowledge and to create a business around your love of health and wellbeing is to launch an online personal training business. The following are the steps to start:

Step 1: Get certified
Before you can start working with clients as a personal trainer, you will need to get certified through a reputable organization such as NASM, ACE or ISSA.

Step 2: Choose your niche
Decide what kind of personal training you want to specialize in. This could be anything from weight loss and bodybuilding to prenatal fitness and senior fitness.

Step 3: Create a website
Your website will be the hub of your online personal training business. Make sure it includes information about your services, rates and credentials. Consider creating a blog to share fitness tips and insights.

Step 4: Build an online presence
In addition to your website, you will need to build a presence on social media platforms like Instagram and Facebook. Share pictures and videos of your workouts and promote your services to your followers.

Step 5: Set your rates
Decide how much you will charge for your personal training services. Consider offering different packages at different price points to appeal to a variety of clients.

Step 6: Create a workout program
Develop workout plans for your clients based on their individual fitness goals and needs. Consider using an online platform like Trainerize to create and deliver your programs.

Step 7: Market your services
Use social media and other online marketing channels to promote your personal training business. Consider offering a free consultation or trial workout to attract new clients.

Step 8: Provide excellent service
Make sure you provide excellent service to your clients to keep them coming back and recommending you to others.

Examples of successful online personal training businesses:

Fit Body App by Anna Victoria: Anna Victoria is a certified personal trainer and fitness influencer who has built a successful online personal training business through her Fit Body App. Clients can access customized workout plans, nutrition guidance and community support through the app.

Sweat with Kayla by Kayla Itsines: Kayla Itsines is another fitness influencer who has built a successful online personal training business through her Sweat with Kayla app. Clients can access workouts, meal plans and community support through the app.

Natacha Océane: Natacha Océane is a personal trainer and YouTuber who has built a successful online personal training business through her YouTube channel and website. She offers customized workout plans and nutrition guidance to her clients.

Jeff Nippard: Jeff Nippard is a professional bodybuilder and fitness coach who has successfully built an online personal training business through his YouTube channel and website. He offers evidence-based training and nutrition advice, and his platforms feature a variety of programs, from strength training to body recomposition. Jeff's approach is scientific and educational, and he's known for breaking down complex topics to make them more understandable.

In conclusion, starting an online personal training business can be a fulfilling and rewarding experience for fitness enthusiasts looking to turn their passion into a business. By following the steps outlined above, you can create a strong foundation for your business and attract clients from around the world. Remember to stay focused on your niche, provide excellent service and use marketing strategies to build your online presence. With hard work and dedication, you can create a successful online personal training business that helps people achieve their fitness goals and improve their overall health and wellbeing.

In the convenience of your own home, starting an online yoga class company can be a wonderful opportunity to spread your love of yoga and assist others in growing their practice. The following are the steps to start:

Step 1: Develop your yoga skills

As an online yoga instructor, it's important to have a strong foundation in yoga and be able to teach various poses and breathing techniques. You can consider taking a yoga teacher training course or advanced yoga workshops to improve your skills.

Step 2: Choose your niche

Decide on what type of yoga you want to teach and who your target audience is. You can focus on beginners, prenatal yoga, restorative yoga or advanced yoga practices.

Step 3: Set up your business

Register your business and decide on a business name. Create a website where you can promote your classes and services. You may also want to set up a social media account to attract more clients.

Step 4: Invest in equipment

To provide high quality online classes, you'll need some equipment such as a good camera, microphone, lighting and a reliable internet connection. You may also need props such as blocks, straps and blankets.

Step 5: Create your classes

Plan and create your classes and make sure to record them in advance. You can use software like Zoom, Skype or Google Meet to conduct live classes or upload pre-recorded classes on your website or social media.

Step 6: Promote your classes

Use social media, email marketing and word of mouth to promote your classes. You can also offer free trials and discounts to attract more clients.

Examples of successful online yoga businesses are:

Yoga with Adriene: With over 10 million subscribers on YouTube, Adriene Mishler has become one of the most recognized online yoga instructors in the world. She offers a range of free yoga videos on her channel that are suitable for beginners and experienced practitioners alike.

Yoga with Kassandra: Kassandra Reinhardt is another popular online yoga instructor who offers a variety of classes ranging from yin yoga to power yoga. Her YouTube channel has over 550,000 subscribers and she also offers online courses and workshops.

Brett Larkin Yoga: Brett Larkin is a certified yoga instructor who offers online classes, courses and retreats. She has over 400,000 subscribers on YouTube and offers a range of practices, including vinyasa flow, meditation and breathwork.

Boho Beautiful: A yoga and travel adventure channel run by Juliana and Mark, Boho Beautiful has gained widespread recognition for its serene yoga sessions set against the backdrop of some of the world's most breathtaking locations. With millions of followers across various platforms, they offer yoga classes, guided meditations, and positive lifestyle content.

In conclusion, starting an online yoga business can be a fulfilling way to share your love of yoga with others while also building a profitable business. By developing your yoga skills, choosing your niche, setting up your business, investing in equipment, creating your classes and promoting them through various marketing channels, you can attract a wide range of clients and provide them with a high quality yoga experience from the comfort of their own homes. With dedication and hard work, you can build a successful online yoga business that brings health and wellness to people all around the world.

A fun and satisfying way to share your love of cooking and teach people new techniques in the kitchen is to launch an online cooking school. Here are some guidelines for starting an online cooking school:

Step 1: Identify your niche
Decide what type of cooking classes you want to offer. Will you teach general cooking skills or focus on a specific cuisine or diet (e.g. vegan, gluten-free, etc.)? Will you offer live or pre-recorded classes?

Step 2: Plan your curriculum
Once you have identified your niche, plan out your course curriculum. Determine what topics you will cover and what recipes you will teach. Make sure to create detailed lesson plans for each class.

Step 3: Choose your platform
Decide where you will host your classes. There are many options for hosting online classes, such as Zoom, Google Meet, Skype or a dedicated platform like Teachable or Kajabi.

Step 4: Invest in equipment
Invest in quality cooking equipment and a reliable camera and microphone for filming your classes. Make sure you have proper lighting and a clean organized cooking space.

Step 5: Set your pricing
Decide how much you will charge for your classes. Consider factors like the length of each class, the complexity of the recipes and the cost of ingredients.

Step 6: Promote your classes
Use social media, email marketing and other online channels to promote your classes. Create a website or landing page where people can learn more about your classes and sign up.

Step 7: Launch your classes
Once you have everything in place, it's time to launch your classes. Start with a few classes and solicit feedback from students to improve your classes and make them even better.

Examples of successful online cooking class businesses include:

MasterClass: This platform features cooking classes taught by celebrity chefs like Gordon Ramsay, Alice Waters and Thomas Keller, among others.

The Rouxbe Cooking School: This platform offers professional-level online cooking courses for individuals and culinary schools.

Plant-Based Cooking: This platform specializes in vegan cooking classes and meal plans to help people transition to a plant-based diet.

The Institute of Culinary Education: This platform offers online cooking classes taught by professional chefs. It caters to both recreational cooks and those looking to develop their skills professionally.

Remember, building a successful online cooking class business takes time, effort and dedication. With a passion for cooking and a willingness to learn, you can create a thriving business that helps people improve their cooking skills and enjoy delicious meals.

Starting an online baking class business can be a fun and rewarding opportunity for those who enjoy baking and want to teach others. Follow the steps listed below to start your own online baking class business:

Step 1: Determine your niche

Decide on the type of baking classes you want to offer, whether it's beginner-level classes, advanced-level classes, classes for kids or classes on specific types of baking such as bread making, cake decorating, pastry making or cookie baking.

Step 2: Create a business plan

Develop a business plan outlining your goals, target audience, marketing strategy, pricing and revenue projections.

Step 3: Create a website

Create a website that is user friendly and looks professional. You can share information about your baking classes and business on the website.

Step 4: Set up your online platform

Choose an online platform that allows you to host and deliver your baking classes, such as Zoom, Google Meet or Skype.

Step 5: Purchase equipment

Buy the necessary baking equipment and supplies that you will need for your classes, such as a stand mixer, baking sheets, measuring cups and spoons, mixing bowls and more.

Step 6: Develop your content

Create a plan for your classes and prepare material like recipes, videos, and handouts for your students.

Step 7: Market your business

Promote your baking classes on social media, your website and through other marketing channels to reach your target audience.

Step 8: Launch your business

Once you have everything in place, launch your online baking class business and start promoting your classes to potential students.

Some examples of successful online baking class businesses include:

King Arthur Baking Company: King Arthur Baking Company is well-respected in the baking community and offers a range of online classes. From beginners to seasoned bakers, there's something for everyone, with courses on bread making, pastries, and other baked goods.

Preppy Kitchen: Run by John Kanell, Preppy Kitchen has made a mark with its extensive baking tutorials suitable for both newbies and expert bakers. The platform offers a mix of recipes and detailed video guides on various baking processes.

Craftsy: Craftsy, although catering to multiple creative domains, stands out with its baking and pastry classes. Taught by professionals, the courses span across cake decorating, artisanal bread making, and more.

Baked by Melissa: Baked by Melissa offers a delightful twist to online baking classes, focusing on bite-sized treats. With their creative and fun approach to baking, you can learn how to make mini cupcakes and other bite-sized desserts through their online classes. Whether you're a novice baker or a dessert enthusiast, Baked by Melissa's classes provide a unique and tasty learning experience. Explore their classes and discover the joy of baking delicious bite-sized creations.

Overall, starting an online baking class business can be a fulfilling and profitable way to share your passion for baking with others. With the right tools, resources and marketing strategy, you can build a successful business and help others learn new baking skills.

If you have a love for teaching and are enthusiastic about art, starting an online drawing class business can be a terrific opportunity for you. Here are some guidelines for starting an online drawing school:

Step 1: Develop your skills
Before starting an online drawing class business, it's important to have a strong foundation in drawing. Make sure you have the skills and knowledge necessary to teach others.

Step 2: Define your niche
Decide on the type of drawing you want to teach. There are many different types of drawing, such as portraits, landscapes, cartoons, etc. Determine your niche and focus on teaching that area.

Step 3: Create a business plan
Develop a business plan that includes your target audience, your marketing strategy, pricing and expenses.

Step 4: Choose a platform
There are various online platforms available that can be used for teaching online drawing classes. Choose a platform that is user-friendly and has features such as video conferencing, screen sharing and recording capabilities. Some popular platforms include Zoom, Skype and Google Meet.

Step 5: Set up your website
Create a website for your online drawing class business. The website should include information about your classes, pricing, schedules and contact information.

Step 6: Create marketing materials:
Create marketing materials such as flyers, brochures and business cards. You can also use social media to promote your online drawing classes.

Step 7: Build your student base
To build your student base, offer free or discounted classes at the beginning. Word of mouth is a powerful tool, so ask your students to refer their friends and family.

Step 8: Continuously improve
Continuously work on improving your teaching skills and keep yourself updated with new drawing techniques and tools.

Examples of successful online drawing class businesses are:

Proko: Proko is a renowned online platform that provides a variety of drawing lessons, from the basics of anatomy and figure drawing to more advanced techniques. Taught by artist Stan Prokopenko, the courses are designed for learners of all skill levels and emphasize foundational skills every artist should know.

Sketchbook Skool: Sketchbook Skool offers online drawing classes taught by professional artists. The courses are designed to help students develop their creativity and artistic skills, regardless of their skill level or experience.

Virtual Art Academy: Virtual Art Academy is an online art school that provides comprehensive training in drawing and painting. The program is designed for serious artists who want to develop their skills and become professional artists.

21draw: 21draw is an online drawing school that offers courses and tutorials from top industry professionals. The courses cover a wide range of topics, including character design, concept art, and digital painting. 21draw also offers a community forum where students can connect with each other and receive feedback on their work.

Starting an online drawing class business requires dedication, hard work and patience, but with the right strategies and approach, it can be a rewarding venture.

Anyone who enjoys music and has teaching talents may find success in starting an online music tutoring business. A step-by-step guide for starting an online music tutoring business is provided below:

Step 1: Determine your niche
Decide on the type of music you want to teach and the instruments you are proficient in. For instance, you can teach piano, guitar, drums or even vocals.

Step 2: Develop a business plan
A business plan will help you identify your target audience, determine your budget, outline your marketing strategies and set realistic goals. You can create a business plan using online templates or hire a professional to help you develop one.

Step 3: Choose a platform
Select an online platform where you will conduct your classes. There are many options available, such as Zoom, Skype, Google Meet and many more. Ensure the platform you choose is secure, easy to use and has features that support your teaching methods.

Step 4: Set up a website
Develop a website that showcases your services, pricing, schedule and contact information. Ensure your website is user-friendly, mobile-responsive and optimized for search engines.

Step 5: Obtain the necessary equipment
To conduct your classes, you will need a computer or laptop, a high-speed internet connection, a webcam, a microphone and appropriate software or applications for teaching music online.

Step 6: Develop your teaching materials
Create lesson plans, exercises and instructional materials that are easy to understand, engaging and suitable for your target audience.

Step 7: Determine your pricing
Decide on the fees you will charge per lesson or per hour. Research the market to ensure your pricing is competitive and fair.

Step 8: Market your services
Develop marketing strategies to reach your target audience. You can use social media, paid advertising and email marketing to promote your online music tutor class business.

Examples of successful online music tutor class businesses:

TakeLessons: TakeLessons offers online music classes for a variety of instruments, including piano, guitar, singing, and drums. The platform employs qualified music teachers and offers flexible scheduling options. They also have a user-friendly online platform that allows for seamless learning and communication between teachers and students.

Lessonface: Lessonface provides one-on-one music lessons online with experienced teachers. The platform offers lessons for a wide range of instruments, as well as voice lessons, music theory, and songwriting classes. They also have a variety of pricing options to fit different budgets.

Musika: Musika offers online music lessons for a range of instruments, including piano, guitar, and drums, as well as voice lessons and music theory. The platform employs highly qualified music teachers and offers a variety of lesson packages to suit different needs and schedules. They also provide students with performance opportunities and recitals.

In conclusion, starting an online music tutoring business is an excellent way to share your love of music and teaching skills with a wider audience. By following the step-by-step instruction outlined above, you can create a successful online music tutoring business that caters to your niche and target audience. It's important to develop a business plan, choose a suitable online platform, set up a user-friendly website, obtain necessary equipment, create engaging teaching materials, determine fair pricing, and market your services through various channels. With dedication, patience, and the right tools, you can turn your passion for music into a thriving online business.

You can share your knowledge and talents with those who are interested in learning by launching an online handyman class business. A step-by-step tutorial for starting an online handyman class business is provided below:

Step 1: Identify your area of expertise
Consider your experience and skills as a handyman and decide which areas you feel comfortable teaching. Some potential topics include plumbing, electrical work, carpentry, painting and general home repairs.

Step 2: Research the market
Look into other online handyman class businesses to see what they offer and how they structure their courses. Consider factors such as pricing, course duration and course materials included.

Step 3: Plan your course content
Based on your area of expertise, plan out the curriculum for your course. Determine the number of lessons and what topics will be covered in each lesson. Consider creating videos, written materials and quizzes to help reinforce the material.

Step 4: Choose a platform
Decide on the platform you will use to host your classes. There are several options, including video conferencing tools like Zoom or Google Meet or online learning platforms like Teachable, Thinkific or Udemy.

Step 5: Create a website
Build a website to promote your business and offer course registration. Include information about your course, your qualifications as a handyman and any testimonials from past students.

Step 6: Market your business
Use social media, online advertising and email marketing to reach potential customers. Consider offering a free trial or discount to get people to sign up for your course.

Step 7: Launch your course
Once you have everything set up, launch your course and start promoting it. Host live sessions, answer questions and offer support to your students throughout the course.

Examples of successful online handyman class businesses are:

The Handyman Startup: The Handyman Startup offers courses and resources for people who want to start their own handyman business. The courses cover everything from pricing strategies and marketing techniques to tools and equipment needed to run a successful business.

Home Repair Tutor: Home Repair Tutor is a website that offers video tutorials and online classes for people who want to learn how to do home repairs and renovations. The classes cover a wide range of topics, including plumbing, electrical work, drywall repair, and more. The website also offers a community forum where students can ask questions and get help from other students and instructors.

DIY University: DIY University offers a variety of online courses and tutorials for DIY enthusiasts and homeowners looking to learn handyman skills. They cover topics like carpentry, plumbing, electrical work, and more. The platform provides step-by-step instructions and video demonstrations to help learners acquire practical skills for home improvement and repairs.

To get started, you'll need a computer, a webcam or camera, a microphone and a reliable internet connection. You may also need tools and materials to create course content, such as video editing software or a website builder. It's also a good idea to have liability insurance to protect yourself in case of any accidents or injuries that may occur during your course.

Starting an online option trading class business can be a rewarding and exciting venture for those with knowledge and experience in the field. Follow the steps listed below.

Step 1: Develop Your Expertise
It's important to have experience and understanding regarding the field of option trading to be successful. Make sure you have a solid base of knowledge in options trading and an understanding of how the market works before starting your business.

Step 2: Your Building Blocks
The next step is to create your course outline. This means deciding on the most important topics and tactics you'll teach in your class. You might need to create instructional materials like slideshows, activities, and maybe quizzes.

Step 3: Choose Your Platform
To deliver your classes online, you will need to choose a platform that will allow you to host live classes, record sessions and distribute materials. Popular options include Zoom, Skype and Google Meet.

Step 4: Market Your Classes
To attract students to your classes, you will need to market your business effectively. Consider using social media platforms such as Twitter and LinkedIn, as well as paid advertising options such as Google AdWords and Facebook Ads.

Step 5: Set Your Pricing
When setting your pricing, consider the value of your course and the level of expertise you bring. You may choose to charge a flat fee for each class or offer subscription-based pricing for access to multiple classes.

Step 6: Launch Your Business
With your curriculum, platform, marketing plan and pricing in place, it's time to launch your business. Host your first class and use student feedback to refine your approach and continue to grow your business.

Examples of successful online option trading class businesses are numerous and diverse, catering to both novice and experienced traders. Some popular options include:

Option Alpha: This platform offers a variety of online courses, webinars, and podcasts covering everything from basic options trading strategies to more advanced techniques. The founder, Kirk Du Plessis, has years of experience in the financial industry and emphasizes a risk-averse approach to trading.

Investopedia Academy: Investopedia, a leading financial education website, offers a variety of online courses, including several on options trading. Their options trading course covers everything from basic concepts to more advanced strategies and includes interactive quizzes and assessments.

Trading Trainer: Trading Trainer is run by professional trader A.J. Brown and offers a range of options trading courses and coaching services. The courses cover a variety of trading strategies, including directional trading, spread trading, and volatility trading, and are designed to help traders of all levels improve their skills and profitability.

In conclusion, starting an online option trading class business can be a profitable venture for those with the necessary expertise and knowledge in the field. By following the step-by-step guide outlined above, you can develop a strong curriculum, choose a suitable platform, market your classes effectively, set reasonable pricing and successfully launch your business. With dedication and commitment to refining your approach, you can attract and retain students, and build a successful online option trading class business.

Using your knowledge to assist other businesses in making wise judgments can be accomplished by starting an internet business that provides market research services. Here are some starting points:

Step 1: Identify your niche
Decide what area of market research you want to focus on, such as consumer behavior, competitive analysis or industry trends. This will help you target your marketing efforts and differentiate yourself from competitors.

Step 2: Develop your services
Determine what services you will offer, such as surveys, focus groups, data analysis or market reports. You may want to specialize in certain types of research or offer a range of services depending on your expertise and target audience.

Step 3: Build your website
Make a website that highlights your expertise and services. Provide detailed information about your services, including pricing and how to contact you. You can also add case studies or testimonials from your previous clients to show your experience.

Step 4: Market your business
Use social media, content marketing and paid advertising to promote your services and reach potential clients. Consider targeting businesses in your niche or offering free consultations to attract new clients.

Step 5: Build relationships
Develop relationships with clients by providing high quality research services and offering ongoing support. This can help you generate repeat business and referrals.

Step 6: Stay up-to-date
Keep up with industry trends and changes in the market research landscape to ensure that your services are relevant and competitive.

Examples of successful online market research services businesses:

SurveyMonkey: SurveyMonkey is a popular platform for conducting surveys and collecting data from customers and employees. They offer a range of survey services that can be customized to meet the needs of businesses of all sizes. Their user-friendly interface and affordable pricing make them an attractive option for companies looking to conduct market research.

Qualtrics: Qualtrics is another leading platform that offers advanced research tools and data analytics. They specialize in helping businesses understand customer experience and employee engagement, among other areas. Their software is used by companies of all sizes, including many Fortune 500 companies.

Nielsen: Nielsen is a global data and analytics company that provides market research services for a range of industries, including media, retail, and consumer packaged goods. They offer a wide range of services, including audience measurement, consumer insights, and marketing effectiveness. With a wealth of experience and a global reach, Nielsen is a trusted partner for many businesses looking to gain insights into the market.

Starting an online market research company can be rewarding for those with knowledge in the industry. To succeed, you must find your target market, develop services, build strong client relationships, advertise effectively, and keep up with industry trends. As the demand for market research services grows, now is a great time to launch your own company and assist businesses in making informed decisions.

For someone with experience in audio production and marketing, starting a podcast production company that provides clients with online editing, recording, and distribution services might be a lucrative business venture. The following are the steps to start:

Step 1: Develop your skills
Before starting a podcast production business, it is important to have experience in audio production, editing and recording. You probably need to take courses or work on some projects to develop your skills.

Step 2: Create a business plan
Writing a business plan can help you set your goals, understand your target market, competition, pricing, and financial projections. Following your business plan will guide your actions and help you reach your goals.

Step 3: Choose a niche
To attract clients who are interested in your services, it's important to focus on a specific podcast niche, like business, sports, entertainment, or education. This will help you concentrate your marketing efforts and find the right audience.

Step 4: Create a website
A website is important for marketing your business and finding clients. You can use platforms like WordPress or Squarespace to build your website. More information about this is provided later in this book.

Step 5: Purchase equipment
You will need quality equipment, including microphones, headphones, editing software and recording software. You can find quality equipment on websites such as Amazon or B&H Photo Video.

Step 6: Set your pricing
Pricing your services can be a challenge. You should research what other podcast production businesses charge for similar services and set your pricing accordingly. You may also want to consider offering package deals for clients who need multiple services.

Step 7: Promote your business
You can promote your podcast production business through social media platforms like Twitter, LinkedIn, and Facebook. These platforms allow you to engage with potential clients and show your work to a wider audience. By consistently publishing high quality content relevant to your niche, you can increase your online presence and draw in more clients.

Step 8: Build relationships with clients

It is important to have good relationships with your clients to make your business successful. You should give great customer service, complete work on time, and surpass expectations.

Examples of successful podcast production businesses include:

Podcast Motor: Podcast Motor provides editing, production and publishing services to podcasters. They offer monthly plans that include a dedicated producer, unlimited editing and podcast optimization.

The Podcast Host: The Podcast Host offers a range of podcasting services, including editing, hosting and production. They also offer training and consulting services for those who want to start their own podcast.

Podfly: Podfly is a provider of personalized podcast production services that include a comprehensive suite of solutions, such as recording, editing, and distribution. The company also specializes in providing additional services, including social media management and graphic design.

Resonate Recordings: Resonate Recordings offers professional podcast production services, including audio editing, mixing, and mastering. They provide assistance with content development, voice-over, and even podcast website design. With a user-friendly client dashboard, they aim to simplify the podcasting process for creators.

Pro Podcast Solutions: Pro Podcast Solutions is a full-service podcast production company that caters to podcasters at all levels. They offer services such as audio editing, show notes creation, and publishing assistance. Additionally, they have a team of experienced podcast editors to ensure a polished final product.

In conclusion, starting an online podcast production business can be a rewarding venture for those with experience in audio production and marketing. By following the steps above, you can establish yourself as a professional podcast producer and attract clients within your niche. It's important to improve your skills, craft a business plan, choose a specific area of focus, build a website, acquire top-notch equipment, set competitive pricing, promote your services, and cultivate strong relationships with your clients. By delivering exceptional services and building a sterling reputation, you can generate repeat business and attract new customers, ultimately securing long-term success within the vibrant podcasting community. With a strong work ethic and a dedicated mindset, your podcast production business can become a valuable asset to your clients and the larger podcasting landscape.

A successful and rewarding internet business idea is launching a web design firm. The actions to take to get started are as follows:

Step 1: Determine your target market
Decide what type of clients you want to work with, such as small businesses, startups or nonprofits.

Step 2: Develop your skills
Learn web design and development skills through online courses, tutorials and practice. Familiarize yourself with popular web design tools and technologies like HTML, CSS, JavaScript, WordPress and Shopify.

Step 3: Build your portfolio
Create a portfolio website showcasing your best work to potential clients. If you don't have any work experience, create mock projects to demonstrate your skills.

Step 4: Set your prices
Determine your pricing structure based on your skill level, experience and market demand. Research what other web designers in your area or niche charge.

Step 5: Market your services
Create a marketing plan to attract clients, using social media, attending networking events and optimizing your website for search engines.

Step 6: Build relationships with clients
Communicate effectively with clients, understand their needs and deliver high quality work on time.

Step 7: Scale your business
As you gain more clients and experience, consider hiring additional staff or outsourcing work to scale your business.

Some popular examples of successful web design businesses include:

Upwork: A leading freelancing platform where web designers can offer their services to clients all over the world. Clients can post their job requirements and receive proposals from designers with the relevant skills and experience.

99designs: A platform where clients can launch design contests and receive multiple designs from different designers. Clients can choose the best design and work with the designer to finalize the project.

Toptal: A platform that connects clients with the top 3% of freelance web designers and developers. Toptal has a rigorous screening process to ensure that only the best designers and developers are accepted into their network.

WebFX: A web design agency that offers custom web design, ecommerce solutions and SEO services. WebFX has a team of experienced designers and developers who work closely with clients to create custom solutions that meet their business needs.

Bop Design: A B2B web design agency that specializes in WordPress websites for businesses across various sectors. Bop Design focuses on creating holistic strategies that encompass brand messaging, content strategy, and lead generation. Their team takes a personalized approach to understand each client's unique business needs and create designs that amplify their brand's essence.

Starting a web design business can be a fulfilling opportunity to transform your passion for design into a profitable venture. With the skills and strategies in place, you can attract clients while growing your business. Determine your target market, develop your skills, and create a portfolio that show your best work. Building strong relationships with clients and delivering top-notch work on time can also help you establish a good reputation and attract repeat business. Staying informed about trends can also help you stay ahead of the game and succeed in this competitive field. By following these steps, you can create a successful web design business that not only meets the needs of your clients but also fulfills your passion for design.

Here are five examples of platforms you may use without any prior knowledge or coding skills to make your own business website:

Wix:

Wix is a popular website builder that allows you to create a website using pre-designed templates. It has a drag-and-drop interface, which is an easy way to build a website. You can also add an online store to your website using Wix's eCommerce features.

Squarespace:

If you're looking for a website builder with visually appealing and mobile-friendly templates, Squarespace is a great option. Their templates offer both style and substance, making it easy to create a professional-looking website.

Weebly:

Create a professional-looking website in minutes with Weebly's pre-built templates and themes. Weebly's eCommerce feature makes it easy to sell your products and services directly on your website.

Shopify:

Shopify is an all-in-one eCommerce platform where you can create an online store easily. With a lot of templates and themes to choose from, you can design your store exactly how you want it. Plus, its simple interface makes managing your store hassle-free, while adding apps can enhance your store's functionality.

WordPress:

WordPress is a popular content management system (CMS) that allows users to create websites with ease. With its wide range of templates and themes, users can easily customize their website's appearance and design. In addition, WordPress offers a plugin called WooCommerce, which enables users to set up an online store to sell products or services. While WordPress is free, users need to pay for hosting and a domain name to make their website accessible on the internet. Adding a plugin like Elementor or Nicepage can further simplify the web design process, even for users without coding experience.

These are just a few examples of platforms that you can use to create your own business website. It's important to do your research and choose a platform that suits your needs and budget.

It can be such an incredible experience starting your own online business. It's a chance to combine making money with doing what you love. Of course, it takes a lot of courage to leave your comfort zone and launch your own business, but it is totally worth it! Being your own boss allows you the freedom and mobility to work from any location and to build a company that represents your values.

If you have recently started your own online business, congratulations on taking the first step towards your dreams! I would love to hear about your journey and share your story with others. Each entrepreneur has a unique story that deserves to be told, and I am eager to help spread the word about your venture.

No matter what type of online business you have started, whether it is an e-commerce store, a blog, a freelance service or any other thing, I am interested in learning more about it. I want to know what inspired you to take the leap and start your own business, how you overcame any obstacles along the way, and what you have learned from your experience.

If your online business is available on the web, I would be happy to take a look at it and potentially feature it on my website, makeitworkforme.com. This way, you could reach a wider audience who may be interested in your product or service, including readers of this book. Being featured on my website could help you gain more visibility and attract new customers or clients.

So, if you have started your own online business after reading this book and want to share your story, please don't hesitate to reach out to me. I am excited to hear from you and help spread the word about your amazing business! Your story could inspire others to take action towards their own entrepreneurial dreams, and I am honored to be a part of that journey.

makeitworkforme.com

GOOD LUCK!